FREE BOOKS

www.*forgottenbooks*.org

You can read literally <u>thousands</u> of books
for free at www.forgottenbooks.org

(please support us by visiting our web site)

Truth may seem, but cannot be:
Beauty brag, but 'tis not she;
Truth and beauty buried be.

To this urn let those repair
That are either true or fair;
For these dead birds sigh a prayer.

Bacon

Charles Larpenteur

Fort Union

FORTY YEARS A FUR TRADER

ON THE

UPPER MISSOURI

THE PERSONAL NARRATIVE

OF

CHARLES LARPENTEUR

1833-1872

EDITED, WITH MANY CRITICAL NOTES,

BY

ELLIOTT COUES

MAPS, VIEWS, AND PORTRAITS

IN TWO VOLUMES

Vol. I

NEW YORK

FRANCIS P. HARPER

1898

CONTENTS.

CHAPTER VI.

(1835-36.)

FORT UNION: CONTINUED.

CHAPTER VII.

(1836-38.)

FORT UNION: CONTINUED.

CHAPTER VIII.

(1838.)

ROUND TRIP TO THE STATES.

CHAPTER IX.

(1838–42.)

COMPOSED OF ALL SORTS.

CHAPTER X.

(1843–44.)

WINTERING AT WOODY MOUNTAIN.

CHAPTER XI.

(1844-45.)

CARNIVAL OF CRIME.

CHAPTER XII.

(1845-46.)

POPLAR RIVER CAMP.

LIST OF ILLUSTRATIONS.

VOL. I.

INTRODUCTION.

HUMAN documents are always interesting, and those which attest the development of the Great West will claim rightful place in literature till the final word concerning that to which they relate shall have been spoken. Such finality in Western history is still afar; it is to be attained by none now living. The field of research is much too wide; and if it be not exactly virginal, nor even have lain quite fallow, the workmen are as yet too few to gather in the immense outstanding crop. The history of what Transmississippian State or Territory has been brought fully up to date? That of not one. Young as most of them are in comparison with a Massachusetts or a Virginia, some are older by far than their reputed ancestors; Arizona and New Mexico had quite a literature before any Plymouth Rock or Jamestown acquired a place on map or in mind. Reviewing what has been done already for the better settled side of the great river, I am oppressed by a sense of the story yet to be told of the " biggest half " of the American commonwealth. Now is none too early to cease to be inarticulate in the parts we have to perform; for the plot thickens and the setting of the stage is splendid. Let us speedily utilize our properties; they are readily accessible, and they abound; they should not be suffered to lapse with fugacious years in the insatiable maw of Time the cosmic cannibal, the ceaseless corroder and obliterator, alike the progenitor of all things and their relegator to forgetfulness.

Lest we too may forget, I wish to do my share as a curator of historical materials, even if I may not aspire to the office of historian. Among my beliefs is that of the prime utility of contemporaneous documents for historical purposes. These are the great antiseptics to the ptomaines of tradition—the stocky facts so fatal to mythopoetic microbes. Much history so called may be the Carlylese "distillation of rumors," or the Napoleonic "fable agreed upon"; but much more may be relieved of any such imputation if we do our duty by our documents. It would surprise most persons to realize how quickly a neglected core of fact gathers the mold of myth. Take the Lewis and Clark expedition, for example. Never, perhaps, was a true story more minutely and completely told; to know all about it, we have only to read what the explorers themselves had to say, less than one hundred years ago. But the take-it-for-granters, the forsoothers, the forgetters, the prevaricators, the misquoters, the unreaders—the whole tribe of quidnunc impressionists—have meanwhile found out more things that never happened in this case than they ever learned about what did happen. According to such authorities, there are few early years of this century in which Lewis and Clark were not traveling; fewer routes they did not take across the continent; and fewest of all are the places in the Rocky mountains where they did not pass one or two winters. Many persons who live in the shadow of Pike's Peak never knew the initials of his name; some think he was Albert Pike, the great Freemason; some never thought anything about it; and nearly all suppose that one Pike discovered and surmounted the peak which bears his name. Yet anyone who should take the trouble to consult the very original document which Pike himself has handed down to us would learn all there is to be known on that particular point.

The history of the West is still largely the story of discovery, exploration, survey, colonization, and the like; for aught else is of comparatively recent development—is contemporaneous, or nearly such. The bison was the original engineer, who followed the lay of the land and the run of the water; the Indian followed the bison; the white man followed the Indian; the gun and trap, the pick and shovel, the whiskey-jug, plow, and locomotive followed the white man, at little if any interval: this is the order of empire westward. Every step of this succession is of absorbing interest and momentous consequence; perhaps none more so than those taken during what I may style the picturesque period, when the plain was furrowed not by the plow but by the hoof of the bison, when no Indian war-whoop had been silenced by a steam-whistle, when the trapper and trader were romantic figures in scenes untamed to more prosaic industries. Such times as these call for chroniclers; and it is the purpose of the AMERICAN EXPLORER SERIES, of which the present volumes form a continuation, to traverse this historic ground, perhaps to cultivate some corners of this fruitful field. What results may be expected are instanced in the case of the Journal of Jacob Fowler, with which the series began. Whoever heard of it, or of its author, till this year of grace 1898? A floating paragraph in one or two not well-known books was to the vague effect that a trader named Glenn took a party to Santa Fé in 1822—that was all. Now we have the narrative of that enterprise, complete in every detail, in an authentic, genuine, original, contemporaneous human document—and of such is the kingdom of history.

Few persons now living may measure the full importance of the Fur Trade as a factor in the development of what has been called the "wild and woolly West"—thereby giving occasion for Lummis' witty retort upon a "tame and cottony East." Fewer still can be aware of what iniquities and atrocities the seamy side of that indispensable industry reveals. Those who have read the Journals of Alexander Henry and David Thompson have had their eyes opened to the systematic swindling and debauching of Indians which characterized the traffic as conducted in Canada and some portions of the United States, and may readily believe that the pursuit of pelf in pelt was always tarred with the same stick. This identical subject—intrinsically important, in some respects repellent, never failing of tragic interest, albeit sordid and squalid—is continued in the autobiography of Charles Larpenteur.

As Fowler's Journal and Fowler himself were until this year, so have Larpenteur and his narrative been hitherto—unknown. The latter, like the former, will be found composed of the very fiber that goes to the web of history. It is a notable and entirely novel contribution to our knowledge of the Fur Trade of the Upper Missouri for a period of more than an average lifetime, by one who lived the life and worked his way through it, from the position of a mere hand to that of one of its heads. Among other conclusions we may draw from this narrative, it would appear that the unpalliated and unmitigated evils were inherent in the system of traffic itself, red and white natures being what they respectively were; that there was a smoother than the seamy side of the business; that a good, kindly man might be about it, and die poor but honest; and that it called out some of the best as well as the worst of human qualities—some of the most manly, even heroic, traits, remote from cupidity and cruelty.

The circumstances under which Larpenteur's manuscript came into my possession are to be here noted. One day in 1872, when my friend and then brother-officer of the medical corps of the army, Dr. Washington Matthews, was at Fort Buford, he received from the author a letter, the material portions of which I copy literally from the original now before me, as follows:

Little Sioux March the first. 1872
Doctr
     Washington Mathew
                    Dear Sir
                         Your kind favor was received
on the 29th ult. And was pleased to learn that you was well as well as all the folks, and that Buford was progresing so fast. I would like very much to see the old place again. I Cannot take any more Comfort down here, particularly after the death of my little boy. . .
     But a few days ago I got through writing a book of my life, by this title—History—
                    of the life of Charles Larpenteur. With

many interesting Stories written by himself, after the residence of fourty years in the Indian Country Also his views on Indian affairs and sugestions for their governement

I intended to have this work publishd but it will Cost me more than I Can afford I have tried some in Sioux City, they say it will Cost $1.25 per page, to get it ready for the print, now there Comes the printing, binding, and illustrations, it would amount to at least $500. not knowing whether it would take. This manuscript would be of some use to you, if you whish I will send it up to you, you Can look it over and tell me what you think of it. I think also that you Coud get it up in good shape for the print I would satisfy you well for your trouble. It will Contain about three hundred pages, a book the size of Ecy, omo [Ecce Homo] . . . I have the honor to remain very respectfully

Yours

[signed] Chas Larpenteur

After some further correspondence, the original manuscript of this " History of the Life of Charles Larpenteur," etc., making about two hundred closely written foolscap pages, was mailed to Dr. Matthews by its author, on June 14, 1872. A clerical copy was made, and the original returned to its owner. This copy was kindly placed in my hands by Dr. Matthews, at Washington, D. C., on Oct. 17, 1897, for any use I might wish and be able to make of it. I soon afterward received the original from Mr. A. L. Larpenteur, of St. Paul, Minn., a nephew of the author; and through the friendly attentions of Mr. Mitchell Vincent, of Onawa, Ia., I was further favored with various other of Larpenteur's autograph journals and note-books which had been found in the possession of his widow at Fontainebleau, near Little Sioux, Ia. Such are the first-hand materials upon which the present work has been prepared for publication; and thus has been realized the desire of the author's heart, a quarter of a century after it ceased to beat.

Larpenteur seems to have cherished aspirations beyond his powers of accomplishment; his ambition outran the strict limitations of his frontier environment, so untoward authorship. He was fond of himself, as most persons are, and doubtless found in the pen a last means of relieving the uneasy introspection consequent upon financial failure, ill health, and other grievous burdens. But he journalized more or less from beginning to end of his adult life, the principal events of which he faithfully set forth, according to his lights, in the final "History" which he completed a few months before his death.

Dr. Matthews, who knew Larpenteur personally, describes him to me as a small, spare, wiry man of distinct Gallic type, as shown in the photographic frontispiece of this volume. He was very intelligent, vivacious and witty in conversation, full of anecdote and reminiscence, and unusually well-informed for a man in his position. He was also fairly well-read, which may have made him a full man, though his reading never enabled him to acquire any considerable facility or felicity of expression in writing. Notwithstanding his habitual handling of the pen, he was never on good terms with English orthography and syntax. This does not seem to have been due to his nationality; English so early took the place of his mother tongue that it is not probable he could have written better, if as well, in French. Indeed, the rarity of a French phrase or word in his writings is notable, and there is hardly a trace of foreign idiom in the composition of this *Français de France*.

In disposition Larpenteur was kindly and amiable, though quite capable of harboring resentment against any who had ruffled his quick plumes or wounded his amour-propre. Personal vanity was no doubt his foible, as it is that of most Frenchmen, and a great many other people. *That* once wounded was hard to heal, perhaps never quite cured; and when unhurt it often made him consider himself a more important factor in the universe than the facts may have seemed to others to warrant. But he had marked ability in his business and was considered a safe and sure man, who could be implicitly trusted, even by those who did not like him personally; his integrity was questioned by none. This is a characterization given me by more than one person of whom he speaks disparagingly in his book, and whose good opinion in this particular I trust will not be modified by anything he has written. I think myself that he has been, no doubt unintentionally, unjust in one or two instances I could cite; but I have not felt at liberty to materially modify any expression of his sentiments. These are in the nature of quit-claims to some old scores, not open to reconsideration since the mortgage has been foreclosed by death.

"The journalist," as he often styled himself, took pride in his personal appearance, and liked to adorn it. He was very courteous in address, never addicted to profane or indecent language, and seldom drank—never to excess. All this was quite enough to set him apart unpleasantly from most of his associates, and make him a sort of white crow or black swan to the half-horse, half-alligator individualities of that Missourian fraternity among whom his lot was cast. His courage was rather of the moral than of the physical kind, and therefore viewed with unconcern by the average dare-devil of his entourage. Unlike most of his white companions he had no dull indifference to theology; he took an inquisitive interest in such speculations, and became an unbeliever in church creeds and dogmas. He found in salutary cynical philosophy a refuge from the many reverses and misfortunes he experienced; and his final financial ruin in the business to which he had devoted the best years of his life had made him a practical pessimist by the time he wrote his memoirs. A Voltairish undertone runs through them; he seems to be always greeting the inevitable with a shrug, and soothing his self-love to the last by shifting the blame on fate—as much as to say, I must have been born to bad luck, else how explain this result of all my industry, ability, and other commendable qualities? He was a man who made warm friends, and enemies of like temperature; those who knew him best were most likely to be the former. As for the latter, we must remember the significant fact, that almost every native American on the Upper Missouri hated a Frenchman on general principles, as a matter of race-prejudice hardly possible to overcome.

But of all such things, and others that might occupy the remainder of this Introduction, the discerning reader will be able to judge as well as the editor, upon sufficient scrutiny of the full-length portraiture Larpenteur has naïvely left of his individuality. The editor need not say much of his share in the net result, as it consists chiefly in polishing and hanging appropriately the mirror in which Larpenteur viewed his own likeness. The author was aware of his literary infirmity when he sent the manuscript to Dr. Matthews, thinking that the latter " could get it up in good shape for the print "; and this is what I have tried to do. The writing was not bad enough to preserve inviolate as a curiosity, like Jacob Fowler's; yet there was scarcely a sentence in it all that did not need to be recast to some extent in preparing the manuscript for publication. But this is a mere matter of grammar; I have simply helped the author to express himself; the sense and sentiment are his own, if the style is not.

Readers of Larpenteur will judge of his ability as a raconteur. Of his truthfulness there is no question. He has given us a very notable contribution to the history of the West—one with which future writers upon his time and scene must reckon. I am sure that this is a book of which it may be said, in the mother tongue of a Montaigne, "*cecy est un livre de bonne foy.*"

Dr. Washington Matthews, who generously relinquished to me his copy of the original manuscript, is further to be credited with no small share of the editing, annotating, and illustrating of these volumes. I make more formal acknowledgment to him on a preceding page; here I have the pleasure of witnessing his kind assistance throughout the work. In reading the proofs with me he has always given me the benefit of his long experience on the Upper Missouri, of his keen criticism and wise counsel: so that, if any points be left obscure or dubious, it is because our united intellects were unequal to the emergency. I am also particularly indebted to Mr. Mitchell Vincent for placing much valuable material in my hands, including a map of Fontainebleau and vicinity, which he drew for this work; and to Lieutenant Colonel H. M. Chittenden, Corps of Engineers, U. S. A., for many friendly attentions and valued suggestions during the progress of the work. I have also been assisted in various ways by Mr. A. L. Larpenteur and Mrs. Charles Larpenteur; Mr. Henry A. Boller, of Denver, Col., who has taken in such good part certain strictures which will be found in his quondam partner's text; Hon. Charles Aldrich, of the State Historical Department, Desmoines, Ia.; Mr. John H. Charles, of Sioux City, Ia.; Mr. D. W. Butts, of Little Sioux, Ia.; Mr. D. W. Longfellow, of Minneapolis, Minn.; Rev. C. L. Hall, of Elbowoods, N. Dak.; Mr. W. O. Owen, of Cheyenne, Wyo.; Mr. Maurice Kingsley, of New Rochelle, N. Y.; Mr. F. W. Hodge, of the U. S. Bureau of Ethnology at Washington, D. C.; General O. B. Willcox, U. S. A.; Prof. Asaph Hall, of Cambridge, Mass.; Ex-President Benjamin Harrison, of Indianapolis, Ind.; and Miss Helen P. Clarke, of the Otoe Agency, Okla. The extensive Index, which renders immediately accessible every capitalized name to be looked for in the book, and various other subjects, has been prepared by Mrs. Mary B. Anderson with the same skill and care she has shown in several previous instances.

E. C.

No. 1726 N Street, Washington, D. C.,
October 17, 1898.

LARPENTEUR'S AUTOBIOGRAPHY.

CHAPTER I.

(1807-33.)

MY PARENTAGE AND EARLY LIFE.

IN order to inspire the reader with confidence in the veracity of my writing—for it must be borne in mind that I write this book for true and faithful information of the public—I thought it would be well to give him an introduction to myself, before entering on the journey.

I was born in France, in the year 1807,[1] five miles from Fontainebleau, on the border of the beautiful Seine, 45 miles from Paris. My father, who was neither rich nor poor, but a great Bonapartist, left France for America immediately after the battle of Waterloo, thinking that the American government

---

[1] Date of birth at variance with the inscription on his tombstone, which states that he died Nov. 15, 1872, aged 69 years, 6 months, 7 days.

would make some attempt to get Napoleon off the island of St. Helena; but after conversing with several individuals, and particularly with Commodore Porter,[2] he found that the government would countenance no such attempt.   So the project was abandoned—I say the project, for it had been started by the many French officers who were at the time in Philadelphia. Louis XVIII. having issued a pardon, most of them returned to France.   My father returned after an absence of one year, during which he found the American government and the country to suit him.   So he sold all his property and left France in 1818, with a family of four children—three boys and one daughter, I being the youngest son.   In his travels in America he had chosen Baltimore as his future residence. Having landed at New York we came to Baltimore, where he purchased a small farm of 60 acres, five miles from the city.   This farm belonged to some French who had been forced to emigrate by the massacre of St. Domingo, and was established by Monsieur La

[2] David Porter, the distinguished American naval officer, father of Admiral David Dixon Porter, b. Boston, Feb. 1, 1780, d. Pera, Turkey, Mar. 3, 1843.   At date of the battle of Waterloo, June 18, 1815, and thereafter to Dec., 1823, Capt. or Comm. Porter was a member of the board of naval commissioners.   He resigned from the navy in 1826, had command of the naval forces of Mexico in 1826-29, was consul-general of the United States to Barbary for a year or more, and finally U. S. minister to Turkey, 1831-43.

Bié Du Bourgh De Berg [*sic*]; it was well supplied with fruits, but the soil was poor and stony, and this lad got sick of it. Hearing much of the fine rich soil of Missouri, I determined to try my luck in the Far West—for at that time it was considered quite a journey to St. Louis.

So at the age of twenty-one I determined to leave home, and started with a gentleman by the name of J. W. Johnson, who had been a sutler at Prairie du Chien, and had a large number of negroes whom he was taking to Missouri. I assisted him as far as Wheeling, where he took a steamer, and I went across country on horseback alone. That is 43 years ago. I had a fine trip of 22 days. I remained two years about St. Louis in the capacity of overseer for Major Benjamin O'Fallon,[3] a retired Indian agent, with whom I had a great deal to talk about Indians and

[3] Son of Dr. James O'Fallon and Frances Clark (sister of William Clark and afterward Mrs. Thruston), and brother of Col. John O'Fallon: see Lewis and Clark, ed. 1893, pp. lxv, lxxx, xci. " Benjamin O'Fallon was for many years an Indian Agent of the United States. He was an honest, courageous, and careful officer, who possessed great influence over the various tribes with whom he came in contact, and was of great service in aiding the government in many treaties. His memory is perpetuated in the West by O'Fallon's Bluff on the Platte River in Nebraska, and O'Fallon's Creek in Montana, near Glendive," Cont. Hist. Soc. Montana, ii, 1896. p. 227. For other names of O'Fallon's creek, tributary to the Yellowstone, see L. and C., ed. 1893, p. 1163.

Indian countries, which finally induced me to try the wilderness.

My first trip was up the Mississippi to Des Moines rapids, the year previous to the Black Hawk War of 1832. At this time there were two stores at Keocuck [4]—not yet called by that name; one of them belonged to an individual named Stillwell,[5] and the other to Mr. Davenport,[6] who was afterward murdered on

---

[4] Keokuk, Lee Co., Ia., was chiefly known as The Point in 1831, but also called Foot of the Rapids, and Puckeshetuck, until it was christened after the celebrated Sac chief whose name it still commemorates. The proposal to call it Keokuk appears to have been first made by Col. George L. Davenport, at a meeting held to celebrate July 4, 1829, on a steamboat then lying at what is now the foot of Main st.: so Dr. Isaac Galland, in a letter published some years before his death in 1858, quoted in Hist. Lee Co. There is a conflict of dates here; Isaac R. Campbell states that there was no Ke-O-kuk till 1835, when the name was proposed by some steamboat men detained there to lighten over the rapids: but the original proposal and final adoption of the name may easily have been at different dates. "From this time"—1835, says Mr. Campbell—"the name of Keokuk was adopted, and, in 1837, I sold my potato-patch enclosure to Dr. Isaac Galland, Agent of the New York Land Company, and, under his supervision, a city in embryo was formally inaugurated and recorded as 'Keokuk.'" The first house is said to have been built there by Dr. Samuel C. Muir, in 1820; Dr. Galland laid out the original town plat in 1837.

[5] Moses Stillwell, whose daughter Margaret was the first white child born at The Point, Nov. 22, 1829.

[6] Col. George L. Davenport, murdered in his home on Rock Island, by the Fox and Hodges gang, July 4, 1845—the noted

Rock Island. I came up to the place in a small steamer called the Red Rover, commanded by Capt. Throgmorton,[7] who is still alive and has made many trips up this river—as fine a gentleman as I ever knew. On the way up I became acquainted with Mr. Blondo,[8] interpreter for the Sac and Fox Indians. He took a great fancy to me, and nothing would do but I must go with him to his farm, seven miles up the rapids, and remain there until the boat got over the rapids, which it was supposed would take a long time, as the river was very low. I consented, got a horse caloh,[9] and we started. The improvements consisted of a comfortable log cabin, and Blondo was indeed

person for whom the city of Davenport, Ia., was named, and not to be confounded with Col. William Davenport of the U. S. Army, who was some time stationed on Rock Island. His house was still standing in 1890 or later. See Davenport Democrat of Dec. 16, 1890, and Ann. of Iowa, ii, Nos. 2 and 3, July–Oct., 1895, p. 243

[7] Dr. Matthews informs me that Larpenteur's praise of Capt. Throckmorton is none too generous, and adds: "He was an old resident of St. Louis—a steamboat owner who often took command of his own vessels, and hence was called captain. He had a large family, mostly daughters, some of whom must still live in St. Louis. His boat, with himself and family on board, was frozen in at Fort Buford one winter—I think 1870–71. I have met him frequently, but do not remember his first name."

[8] Interpreter Blondeau had been there or thereabouts for many years: see Pike, ed. of 1895, pp. 32, 34, 211, referring to 1805–06.

[9] *Sic*—probably for calash, calesh, or calèche—a sort of one-horse vehicle.

well fixed for the country at the time. After some little time he took me into the village and introduced me to several of the leading men, of whom a great many were drunk, and toward evening he got so drunk himself that he frequently asked me if I did not want to " smell powder," but as I never felt like smelling powder as he proposed, I declined, not knowing why he used the expression. After the spree the old gentleman was very kind, took me all over the half-breed reservation—as fine country as I ever saw—and finally remarked that he would give me all the land I wanted if I should happen to make a match with his niece, Louise Dauphin. That was said after I had given up the idea of going on to Prarie du Chien, where I was bound; but, thinking myself too young, I declined all overtures, although I confess that I came very near accepting the offer, for Louise was one of the handsomest girls I ever saw—it cost me many long sighs to leave her, and more afterward.

After two months' residence at the rapids I returned to St. Louis, with full determination to see more of the wild Indians. General Ashley,[10] who

[10] General William H. Ashley, one of the most enterprising and successful of the St. Louis fur traders, lieutenant governor in 1820-24, member of Congress, etc. His name was a power all over the West in those days. The curious reader will find much about him, and some things very much to the personal point, in James P. Beckwourth's book, *passim:* see, for example, the

was then carrying on great beaver trapping in the Rocky mountains, was in the habit of hiring as many as 100 men every spring. They were engaged for 18 months, to return in the fall of the following year with the furs. Not long after I came from the rapids General Ashley's party returned from the mountains with 100 packs of beaver. A pack of beaver is made up of 60 average beavers, supposed to weigh 100 lbs., worth in New York at that time from $7 to $8 per lb. It is impossible to describe my feelings at the sight of all that beaver—all those mountain men unloading their mules, in their strange mountain costume—most of their garments of buckskin and buffalo hide, but all so well greased and worn that it took close examination to tell what they were made of. To see the mules rolling and dusting is interesting and shocking at the same time; most of them, having carried their burdens of 200 pounds' weight for about 2,000 miles, return with scarcely any skin on their backs; they are peeled from withers to tail, raw underneath from use of the surcingle, and many are also lame.

William Sublette[11] and Robert Campbell[11] had

redoubtable Jim's quarrel and reconciliation with him, pp. 57–68 of C. G. Leland's ed., 1892.

[11] Each a well-known person in the fur trade, of whom we hear much in the sequel. In 1833 they were partners in the Rocky Mt. Co., and their trip to the mountains in 1832, when they were

attended General Ashley on several trips to the mountains—Campbell as clerk, mostly on account of his health; he had previously been clerk for Keith and O'Fallon.[12]   Sublette was a farmer near St. Louis, but was more for trapping beaver than farming.

The sight of all this made me determined to take a trip of the same kind.   The journey to the Rocky mountains at that early period was considered very hard, and dangerous on account of the Pawnees and Blackfeet.   While trapping that summer William Sublette had been badly wounded in the shoulder in a fight with the Blackfeet.[13]   But not all this danger, and the hardships to be endured on such a trip, could prevent me from engaging, in the spring of 1833.[14]

accompanied by N. J. Wyeth's party, will be found noted in Irving's Bonneville, chap. vi.

[12] Col. John O'Fallon: see note [3], p. 3.

[13] The battle of Pierre's Hole, 1832, which became well-known by Irving's spirited description in his Bonneville, chap. vi, where Sublette's wound in the shoulder is noted.

[14] The Autobiography had here: " As near as I can remember in the spring of thirty-two 1832." But Larpenteur's memory was then at fault; the date is 1833. This is proven by his Original Journal, which he began to write at Fort Union on Sept. 8, 1834, and which is now before me. It opens thus: " Fort Union Missouri Mouth of the Yellow Stone September the 8 1834 Being always desirous to visit the Rocky Mountains and not being able to satisfy my curiosity by means of cash I was obliged to hire to Mr Sublette & Campbell has [as] a common hand to protect there

I first provided myself with a good recommendation from Major Benjamin O'Fallon, who was well
known for his integrity, and would give no one a
recommendation unless he deserved it.   Provided
with this document I next made application to the
American Fur Company, which was then carried on
by P. Chouteau and Co.   J. J. Astor was still in the

goods and all that appertained to the said Sublette and Campbell
to the risk of our lives indangered by Indians and all other axi-
dents. wee left the City of Saint Louis on the 13th of April |1833|,"
etc.—the date interlined and framed in a rectangle to make it
more conspicuous, as here printed.   Larpenteur then goes on to
give an orderly account of consecutive incidents as they occurred
in 1833 and 1834, till he thus "catches up " to his date of writing
in 1834.   As his memory was then fresh, and as there is no break
in sequence of events, it is clear that 1833 is the date of his start
from St. Louis—though why he did not refresh his failing memory by referring to his own Journal can hardly be imagined.
Dates are infrequent in the greater part of the Autobiography,
but toward its close they recur regularly, showing that Larpenteur had before him a journal of these later years.   We shall
have frequent occasion to challenge or check his Autobiography,
written so late in life, by means of his old Journals, four of
which I possess; and shall sometimes weave into his present
narrative materials derived from the same authentic sources.
    Our start in 1833 is confirmed by various other data, of which
I select two : 1. Bonneville first crossed the plains in 1832, wintered 1832-33 in the mountains, and met Larpenteur's party at
the Green River rendezvous in July, 1833. 2. Larpenteur in his
Journal, as above, accounts continuously for events of 1833-34 to
Nov. 30, which he gives as date of an eclipse of the sun, which I
have ascertained was visible to him on Nov. 30, 1834.

company.   Mr. J. B. Sarpy was at the time the person
who engaged the men.   As I was young, well dressed,
and not a bad-looking lad, but did not seem to be very
robust, he remarked that he did not think I would
answer for his purposes.   I then showed him my
document from the major, whom we both knew well,
and the remark he made was, " Ah, if you had not
deserved this, you would not have gotten it."   Then,
said he, " you are a Frenchman? "   I replied in the
affirmative.   " You have some education," he continued; " why do you want to engage as a common
hand? "   I then told him that my desire was to see
the Rocky mountains, that I was willing to undergo
all the hardships of such a voyage, and that I wished
to start from this place on horseback.   He then re-
ferred me to Messrs. Sublette and Campbell, saying
that, if I engaged with him, I should have to go as
far as Fort Pierre,[16] and there start for the mountains
with Mr. Fontenelle.   Being anxious for an immediate ride, that proposition did not suit me.   I then
went to the office of Sublette and Co., which firm had
bought out all Gen. Ashley's interests in the moun-

[15] Old Fort Pierre, on the right (west) bank of the Missouri, 3
m. above the mouth of Teton or Bad river; so named for Pierre
Chouteau, Jr.—the one whom Larpenteur has already mentioned.
The locality is that of present Pierre, S. Dak., which takes its
name from the long-noted establishment of P. Chouteau, Jr., and
Co., otherwise the A. F. Co.: see L. and C., ed. 1893, p. 131.

tains, and were also making up an outfit to carry on an opposition to all the trading posts of the American Fur Co. on the Missouri; but I did not know this when I first applied to them.   I found Mr. Campbell in his store, and on informing him of my intentions he appeared to have pretty much the same ideas as Mr. Sarpy.   I soon discovered this and showed him my recommendation.   Being very much of a gentleman, he had the politeness to invite me to his office, and there did all he could to make me abandon the idea of taking such a trip, giving me a full description of what I should be likely to undergo.   But nothing could deter me; go I must, and under the promise that he should never hear me grumble, I signed an article of agreement for 18 months, for the sum $296 and such food as could be procured in the Indian country—that excluded bread, sugar, and coffee.

Now I was thus enlisted, ready for service; but Mr. Campbell was kind to me and always did his best to make my situation pleasant.   So he employed me in St. Louis to assist in packing goods for the upper country, and in equipping the men who were getting ready to leave with the mules for Lexington, Mo., to await the arrival of the steamer which was to bring all their goods up to that point, and of the keel boat which was intended to be cordelled or towed as far as Fort Union with goods for the Indian trade.   I was kept in the store until all the outfits had left St. Louis.

April 7th, 1833.[16]—Now, my dear reader, my mule is saddled, bridled, and hitched at the store in Washington avenue, St. Louis, ready to take me to Lexington, to join the party. If you wish to sacrifice all the comforts of civil life, come with me and share what I shall endure—but no! you can do better than that. For a small sum wherewith to purchase this book you can know it all without leaving your comfortable room. So good-by to civilization—not for eighteen months, but for forty years.

Myself and an individual by the name of Redman started in advance of Mr. Campbell, who was to join us at St. Charles. After we had been there two days he arrived with a young man named James Lee, and a little Snake Indian called Friday, who had been adopted by Mr. Fitzpatrick, a trapper in the mountains and afterward an Indian agent—for which tribe I do not recollect. I shall not be able to give exact dates, as I did not expect to ever write a book; but I will endeavor to come as near as possible. We were eight days on our journey from St. Charles to

[16] Copy has 1832: see note [14], p. 9, where it appears from the Orig. Journ. that Larpenteur left St. Louis Apr. 13, 1833. The year is certain, and Apr. 13 is probably nearer than Apr. 7, for the Journal goes on to say that he reached Lexington on Apr. 20.

Lexington; we fared extremely well, Mr. Campbell having treated us like himself wherever we put up.

On the 18th [or 20th] of April we reached Lexington, where we found our party camped in tents, awaiting our arrival. There the sumptuous fares were all over. Mr. Campbell called me up and said, "Charles, I will now assign you to your mess. I have a mess of nine first-rate old voyageurs—French boys from Cahokia—you will be well off with them." I was not quite a stranger to them, having formed acquaintance with some of them before leaving St. Louis; and I am glad to say that they did all they could for me as long as I remained with them. None of those men had any education, and would frequently remark that if I took care of myself I could get into good business. Our fare during our stay at Lexington was not bad; we drew rations like soldiers, and having yet a little pocket money we could add to our provisions considerably. As to our bedding, it was not very soft, for we were not allowed to carry more than one pair of 3-pound[11] blankets. A few days after

[11] More commonly called 3-*point* blankets by traders and trappers whose narratives I have read. The "point" was a short black stripe, about four inches long. woven into the Mackinaw blanket to indicate its weight ; a 3-pound blanket had three such stripes. So a point was a pound in blankets, just as in cooking recipes "a pint's a pound, the world round."

As to the mule-packs of which Larpenteur goes on to speak, his

our arrival mules were given to each of us—two to pack and one to ride. Mr. Campbell gave me his favorite mule Simon to ride; old Simon was not so kind that he would not buck me off his back when he took a notion to do so, but on the whole was a good fellow in comparison with many others. My two pack mules were very gentle, but would kick off their packs sometimes. My two loads consisted of beaver traps and a small top pack—a choice load, not likely to turn over like dry goods. As I was a green hand my mates assisted me a great deal, and I was always thankful to them for it.

Journal is more explicit. "On the 28th," it says, "Our names were taken and our load given us, consisting of liquor Guns Powder led Blanket, Pantaloons Shirts capos [capotes] Beaver Traps and many other artikals too numerous to mention. Three Mules were given me, one for my rideing Animal and the two others for packing. my loads consisted of traps raisins chocolatte."

CHAPTER II.

(1833.)

ON the 12th of May [1] we took our departure for the mountains, and at the same time the keel boat left Lexington landing, manned by thirty men with the cordell on their shoulders, some of them for the distance of about 1800 miles. Our party consisted of 40 [2] enlisted men; Robert Campbell, boss in charge; Louis Vasquez, an old mountain man; Mr. Johnesse, a clerk in charge of the men, whose place it

[1] Date in question: Orig. Journ. makes the start from Lexington Apr. 28, "on the same day" the mule-packs were made up and given out. The first day out they traveled only 5 m., and then waited 3 days for Mr. Sublette, who was coming in a steamboat that was to tow the keel boat as far as Liberty, Mo. "On the 7th of May we left the Settlements and on the 9th at knight was the first knight wee stood guard," etc. Some of the discrepancy is evidently due to difference in date of leaving Lexington and of finally clearing out from the last settlement.

[2] Orig. Journ. agrees nearly, saying: "Our number was 45, which was divided into nine guards four at a relief and one officer which made nine officers of which I was one," etc.

was to remain in the rear to aid in readjusting the loads, which would get out of order, and to have an eye to the whole cavalcade. As guests,[3] were Captain Stewart from England, on a pleasure trip; old General Harrison's son, with the view to break him from drinking whiskey; and Mr. Edmund Christy, of St. Louis.

Now hard times commenced. At first the mules kicking off packs and running away was amusing for those who were all right, but mighty disagreeable for the poor fellows who were out of luck. I had my

[3] Beckwourth says of this party, whom he met near the Bighorn river: "I was introduced to a Captain Stuart, who had figured conspicuously, as I was informed, under the Iron Duke, and was now travelling in the far West in pursuit of adventure; also to a Dr. Harrison, son of the hero of Tippecanoe, and to a Mr. Brotherton, with several other gentlemen, who were all taking a pleasure excursion," Autobiogr., 2d ed., 1892, p. 226. Captain or Sir William Stuart's estate, called Murthly Castle, was on the south side of the Tay in Perthshire, Scotland, running about 4 miles down river from the gates of Dunkeld. In 1862 the castle was rented to Mr. Robert Graham of Glasgow, and Sir William lived at what was known as the Cottage, a pretty house filled with Indian trophies and other curios, overlooking the Tay, about halfway between the Castle and Dunkeld. Mr. Maurice Kingsley of New Rochelle, N. Y., who gives in these particulars in lit., Jan. 18, 1898, adds that he well remembers Sir William in 1862-65, when the nobleman must have been about 70 years of age—slightly over middle height, a trifle bent, spare but broad-shouldered, with long thin hair almost white, square face and restless grayish-blue eyes—very active still, though gouty and

share of this, but it was not to be compared with the troubles of some of my comrades. This kind of kicking up lasted three or four days in full blast; it finally subsided, yet there would be a runaway almost every day. Our fare consisted of bacon and hard-tack—no sugar nor coffee—for three or four days, after which we each received a small piece of sheep meat, as we had a drove [4] to last us until we got into the buffalo. While the sheep lasted we had but that alone. I then commenced to think that what Mr. Campbell had re-

irascible. He published a book about his adventures, the title of which is one of a great many things I do not know.

"Old General Harrison's son," whom Larpenteur characterizes so tersely, was Dr. Benjamin Harrison, son of William Henry Harrison, hero of Tippecanoe, and ninth President of the U. S., Mar. 4–Apr. 4, 1841. On applying to ex-President Benjamin Harrison for further information, I was favored with the following letter, dated Indianapolis, Ind., Dec. 6, 1897: "My Dear Sir: I have your letter of Dec. 2. I had an uncle, Dr. Benjamin Harrison, who died when I was a lad. I have only a faint remembrance of him. He was of a wild and adventurous disposition, participated, I think, in the Texas war of independence, and in a good many other frontier scrapes, but I have no particular knowledge of the events of his life. . . Very truly yours, BENJAMIN HARRISON."

[4] Orig. Journ. has: "the provisions we had consisted in twenty sheeps two loads of Bacon 500 weight of corn meal which was intended to eat until we got to the Buffello this food to be eaten without bread was not very rellishing when I came to be wnead [weaned] of bread I found that I Should soon be satisfyed of my trip"—*i. e.*, would soon have enough of it, with such poor fare.

marked was on the march.[5]   About a week after we
had been under march the guard was established, and
I was appointed an officer. It became the duty of the
officer every third day to post his men around the
camp, as soon as all the animals were brought in and
picketed in the circle of the camp; those men were to
remain quite still at their stations; the officer was to
cry out "All's well" every 20 minutes, and the men
to cry out the same, so as to find out whether they
were asleep or awake.   Should any one fail to reply,
it was then the duty of the officer to go the rounds to
find out the individual, and if caught asleep to take his
gun to the boss' tent; then in the morning he would
be informed of what he had to undergo, which was a
$5 fine and three walks.[6]   The men on guard were
not permitted to move from their stations, as it was
considered dangerous on account of Indians being
known to creep up to camp and watch to shoot some-
one whom they could discover strolling about; so the
officer was more in danger than his men.   The usual
time of guard was 2½ hours.   Having traveled all day,
being obliged to remain quiet at one's post was very
trying on the sleeping organs, and consequently there
would be some poor fellow trudging along on foot

[5] Meaning that what Mr. Campbell had said would happen was
happening.

[6] That is, to go afoot for three days.

almost every day.   Our route, as well as I can remember, crossed the Little and Big Blue rivers and
continued along the south side of the Platte.[1]   I complained, as my messmates did, of the sheep meat, but
they consoled me as well as themselves by speaking of
the fine feast we soon would have on the buffalo, which
they said they would prefer to all the good messes
that could be gotten up in the States.   Three days
after we had reached the Platte the hunters brought
in one evening a load of meat; but the cry of " buffalo
meat! " was heard long before they came in, and there
was great rejoicement in camp.   Sheep meat could
be had very cheap that evening, and it was amusing
to see the cooks hunting their kettles—some cursing
them for being too small, as though it was the poor
kettle's fault for its size; but it was not long before
they found the kettles were large enough.   Then
came trouble—there was no wood to be found about
camp, and all the fuel we could obtain was the stalks
of some large dried weeds, the wild sunflower.   Now

[1] But crossed the Kansas before reaching the Platte, as the party
were on the regular Oregon Trail.   The Orig. Journ. says: " the
first river of any consiquence that we crossed was the Caw river
where there is an agensey for the Caw Indians which is kept by
General Clark relation of old General Clark, superintendent of
the Indian affaires in St. Louis."   Journ. further states that they
crossed the Kansas May 15; camped there 16th and 17th;
decamped 18th; reached the Platte 23d; and continued on 24th.

and then some hungry fellow would bring in a small armful of that kind of fuel, and his first words would be, " Is the kettle boiling? "   Upon being answered in the negative a long string of bad expressions would be heard, the mildest being, " Waugh! I believe that damned kettle won't never boil! "   Thanks to the virtue of sunflower stalks, however, it boiled at last, and every countenance became pleasant at the thought of tasting that much-talked-of buffalo meat. When it was thought cooked by the old voyageurs, preparations were made to dish it out; but, as we had no pans, a clean place was looked for on the grass, and the contents of the kettle were poured out.   All hands seated around the pile hauled out their long butcher knives, opened their little sacks of salt, and then began operations.   But it was not long before bad expressions were again used in regard to the highly praised quality of buffalo meat.   " I can't chew it "—" Tougher'n whalebone "—" If that's the stuff we've got to live on for eighteen months, God have mercy on us! "   For my part I thought about the same, but said nothing; and after I had chewed as long as I could without being able to get it in swallowing condition, I would seize an opportunity to spit it into my hand, and throw it out unseen behind me.   My comrades asked me how I liked buffalo meat; I replied I thought it might be some better than it was, and they said, " Never mind, Larpenteur; wait until we get among the fat cows—then you will see the difference." [8] At this time of the year, in the early part of June, the cows are not fit to kill; for they have their young calves, and are very poor. For several days after this sheep meat would have kept up its price, and perhaps would have risen in value; but none was allowed to come into market, what little there was being reserved for the boss' mess. So we had to go it on buffalo alone; but, thank Providence! we soon got into fine fat cows, and fared well. My comrades had told me that we should now get a sickness called by them *le mal de vache* [9]; it is a dysentery caused by eating too much fat meat alone, and some are known to have died of it. So it was not long after we fared so well on the fat of the land that very bad expressions were used in reference to living on meat alone.

I cannot say that anything of great importance took place during our journey to the rendezvous; but nowadays, when we have a great deal to say in the newspapers about traveling from Sioux City to Fort Randall, I think that I may indulge in a few more

[8] Out West, instead of saying "to know B from a bull's foot," they have it, "to know poor bull from fat cow," as a criterion of discernment.

[9] Literally "cow-sickness."

remarks before I reach Green river.[10]   After crossing
the South fork of the Platte, the only curiosity of
note is Chimney Rock [11]; that part of the country is

[10] Larpenteur will be found on acquaintance to have a dry
humor, and a sly satire, in a good many things he says, not
always evident at first sight.   There was no Sioux City, Ia., till
about the middle of the 50's; Fort Randall, S. D., was not established till 1856; the railroad only pushed into the former in Feb-
ruary, 1868; and the distance between the two places, about 175
miles by boat, much less by land, was of course a mere jaunt in
comparison with the journey our author was making in 1833 to
the rendezvous on Green river, one of the two main forks of the
Colorado of the West, beyond the Continental Divide.   In the fall
of 1872 I reached Sioux City by rail, but took a steamboat on the
Missouri to Fort Randall, to which post I had been ordered as its
medical officer; I was about three days on the boat, Oct. 15–18.

[11] Having come up the main Platte, crossed the S. Platte at the
forks, and continued up the N. Platte, the party has reached
this long-famous landmark, on the S. side of the river, in Cheyenne Co., Neb.   It was one of several less conspicuous mounds
at isolated points along both sides of the river, not far below
Scott's bluffs.   The Orig. Journ. describes it as "a kind of natural monument which the travellers calls the chimney it is seen
in clear weather from the distance of three or four days travel it
represents pricizely a chimney the base of it is in the shape of a
square pointed roof and from the midst of this roof the chimney
puts out from about twenty-five to thirty feet high and appears
to be something like 100 feet high."   This is a much more reason-
able estimate than was often given of the height, some calling it
upward of 500 feet.   There is a picture of it on the full-page
plate opp. p. 38 of the Senate ed. of Frémont's Exped. of 1842, pub.
1845; at which date Mr. Charles Preuss says the marl and
earthy limestone of the chimney were rapidly wearing away, the
whole formation being not over 200 feet above the river.

SIOUX CITY, IOWA, IN 1866.

too well known at present for me to enter into any description of it. From this point to La Ramie's [12] fort nothing took place worth mentioning except the

[12] The personality of this name is now well-nigh forgotten, in speaking of Fort Laramie, Laramie river, Laramie plains, Laramie peak, and Laramie Co., Neb. La Ramie or Laramie (full name not at hand as I write) was one of the first of the Canadian French voyageurs or coureurs de bois to hunt and trap beaver in this part of the world, and was killed by Arapahoes somewhere about the headwaters of the stream which thenceforth has borne his name. In the course of time there have been several different establishments about the mouth of Laramie river, which finally became a long and well-known military reservation of over 50 sq. m. We find Larpenteur speaking of La Ramie's "fort" in 1833; but that is *ex post dicto;* his Journ. simply speaks of fourche la Ramie, which he crossed on a raft of cottonwoods, and his present words mean simply the *site* of the subsequent establishment. I may also mention that J. K. Townsend, with the Wyeth expedition of 1834, speaks of crossing Laramie fork on June 1, when there was nothing on the spot. The first post appears to have been built that year, 1834, by Wm. Sublette and Robert Campbell; this was a mere stockade of logs, with small bastions on two diagonal corners, and the usual living rooms inside; it stood on the very site of the future U. S. Fort Laramie, on the W. bank of Laramie river, 1½ m. above its mouth. Irving's Bonneville says that it was "about three years" after 1832 that Mr. Robert Campbell built the first post at Laramie, "which he named Fort William, after his friend and partner, Mr. William Sublette," no doubt referring to the same original log stockade of 1834, whose name of Fort William must have speedily lapsed, if indeed it was ever current. In 1835 it was bought by Milton Sublette, "Jim" Bridger, and others, who went into business with the A. F. Co., and it immediately became a rendezvous for Oglala Sioux, under the name of Fort John.

overthrow of our long friend Marsh. It happened
that, in traveling through a country thickly settled
with prickly pears, bad luck would have it that a small
particle of one accidentally found itself under the tail
of his riding mule. The poor animal, finding itself
so badly pricked, kicked and bucked at such a rate
that our long friend was soon unsaddled, and thrown
flat on his back in a large bunch of the prickly pears.

By 1836 the pickets were rotting, and the A. F. Co. replaced the
original stockade with an adobe structure, the last traces of
which did not disappear till 1862. With the old pickets also went
the name Fort John, and Fort Laramie the post was always
afterward. It was held by the A. F. Co. till 1849, when it was
sold to the U. S. government, and became a military post in July
of that year, when it was garrisoned by Companies C and D of
the Mounted Rifles under Maj. Winslow F. Sanderson, who had
attained his majority on Jan. 8 of the previous year, and died
Sept. 16, 1853; Capt. (afterward Gen.) William Scott Ketchum
came with Co. G of the Sixth Infantry in August of the same year
(1849). How important a place Fort Laramie was in those years,
and for long subsequently, may be inferred from the fact that in
1850 wagon-trains and other outfits representing an aggregate of
40,000 animals crossed Laramie river below the fort. I have in
hand an unpublished sketch of Fort John; a plate of the adobe
Fort Laramie of 1842 faces p. 40 of Frémont's Report, already
cited. It would be idle to attempt to cite the references to Fort
Laramie which incessantly recur in books, but I may mention
that it was a sort of hdqrs. for the future celebrated historian
Francis Parkman, when, fresh from college, he was knocking
about among the Indians, and making materials for his Oregon
Trail—not one of his works upon which his fame rests most
securely. The best account of the military post, as it was late in

Although he was over six feet in his stockings, the length of his limbs was not enough to reach out of the patch; and there he lay, begging for pity's sake of his comrades, as they passed by, to help him out of his prickly situation. But all he heard in reply to his entreaties was bursts of laughter throughout the company as they passed by, till he was relieved by Mr. Johnesse,[13] who had charge of the rear. I could but

the 60's, is by Dr. H. S. Schell, U. S. A., in Circular No. 4, War Dept., Surgeon General's Office, Washington, Dec. 5, 1870, pp. 345-350, whence I derive some of the data of this note.

[13] I fear this good Samaritan who brought up the rear and did not pass by on the other side must remain anonymous or pseudonymous, as far as his editor is concerned. He seems to be the Antoine Jeanisse of note [1], p. 52 ; but such a name varies from Jeunesse to Johnson in the MSS. before me, and I can make nothing of it. Compare one Auguste Janisse of Frémont's list of his men, Exped. of 1842, p. 9.

Larpenteur is too much concerned for his poor friend Marsh's plight to give some other particulars which belong here, as I find by his Orig. Journ. On crossing La Fourche de La Ramie and traveling 5 or 6 m. to camp on the N. Platte, it appears that "they was three gentlemen which made there appearance in to our camp of which one of them was mr. Frap one of the members of mr. Fitz Patrick trarping company which was going to st Louis to purchase goods with the intention to return to the Mountains in the fall. the following day we moved camp about half a mile where we remained two days during that time mr Frap maid some agreements with mr Campbell on which he bought the outfit with the exeption of ten mules and ten Barrills of liquor and two bales of goods." This Mr. Frapp was a well-known person in the business for many years, though less noted

pity the poor fellow, but, at the same time, his situation excited mirth. There he lay in a large bunch of prickly pears, stretched out as though he had been crucified. Poor Marsh! I shall remember him as long as I live.

On approaching La Ramie's river we discovered three large buffaloes lying dead close together. The party was ordered to stop and form in double line, while the hunters were gone to find out the cause of those buffaloes' deaths, surmising that they had been killed by Indians. They were gone but a little while before they returned, reporting that the animals had been killed by lightning during a storm we had the previous day; so our fears of Indians were removed, and the party resumed their march. We soon reached the [Laramie] river, where we were ordered to dismount and go to work making a boat out of the hides of the buffalo—quite a new kind of boat [14] to

than Fitzpatrick the Broken Hand. Frémont, p. 40, has this item concerning him: " For several years the Cheyennes and Sioux had gradually become more and more hostile to the whites, and in the latter part of August, 1841, had had a rather severe engagement with a party of six whites, under the command of Mr. Frapp. of St. Louis. The Indians lost eight or ten warriors, and the whites had their leader and four men killed. This fight took place on the waters of Snake river, and it was this party, on their return under Mr. Bridger, which had spread so much alarm among my people."

[14] This was the ordinary " bull-boat," as it is called, made of hides stretched over a light framework of sticks, of circular

me. But the boat was made, and the party with all
the goods were crossed over by sunset. The next
day, or the day after, according to custom Mr. Campbell sent Mr. Vasquez with two men to hunt up some
trappers, in order to find out where the rendezvous
would be, and we awaited their return at this place.
They were gone eight days, which time we enjoyed
in hunting and feasting on the best of buffalo meat.
On the arrival of the trappers and hunters [15] a big
drunken spree took place. Our boss, who was a
good one, and did not like to be backward in such
things, I saw flat on his belly on the green grass, pour-
ing out what he could not hold in. Early next morning everything was right again, and orders were given

shape, like a great clothes-basket or deep saucer. Such a boat
was in regular use by the Indians, and is described and figured
by many authors. A specimen may be seen in the U. S. National
Museum, to the fishery exhibit of which it was contributed some
years ago by Dr. Matthews. I think that this is the one figured
in the late Dr. Charles Rau's Prehistoric Fishing. It is not so
well made as some I have seen on the upper Missouri. The
original exploration of the Yellowstone in 1806 was made in bull-
boats: see L. and C., ed., 1893, p. 1172.

[15] Orig. Journ. has : "Mr. Campbell had sent for Mr Fitz
Patrick to come and receive his goods at a place near the Black
Hills the place appointed for the randezvous. . . We remained
three days at the randezvous after which time Mr Fitz Patrick
arived with three men and six mules loaded with Beaver the following day they settled all their affairs and started Mr Frap
with a party of ten men to go and trap amongst the Black Hills
we also left our camp," etc.

to catch up and start. Everything moved quite
smoothly until we reached the Divide,[16] where my

[16] The Continental Divide, at South Pass, near the head of
Sweetwater river, July 2, 1833. Orig. Journ. is much more
explicit than the above meager text. After continuing up the
N. Platte some distance (not given) from Laramie, the party
passed over to the Sweetwater by a route a little off the Platte,
and reached the former river at or near the famous Independence Rock, so frequently mentioned in books of Western travel
and adventure. "The ordinary road leaves the Platte, and
crosses over to the Sweet Water river, which it strikes near Rock
Independence," Frémont, p. 54. Orig. Journ. describes the
rock with some particularity. Five m. above it is the curious
formation known as the Devil's Gate, where the river runs
through a narrow opening, 300 yards long, 35 yards wide, and
400 feet deep: plate of the Gate in Frémont, opp. p. 57. This
appears to be the place that was originally called "The Fiery
Narrows" by the incoming Astorian overlanders, Oct. 31, 1812:
see this date in Irving's Astoria, chap. xlviii. This party of
seven persons descended the Sweetwater part way, having probably struck it below its upper cañon; they were the first of whom
we have any account as being on this river, long before it
received its present name.

In my Henry Journ., 1897, pp. 884, 885, where I discussed the
route of these Astorians, I was inclined to bring them through
South Pass and thus down the whole of the Sweetwater. But in
a review of Astoria which appeared in the N. Y. Nation of Dec.
23, 1897, I say: "Attentive reconsideration of this point induces
us to fetch them from Green River about south-southeast to very
near South Pass—perhaps within twelve or fifteen miles of it—
when they wandered off the Indian trail which would have
brought them through this pass, and kept about southeast until
they had headed the Sweetwater entirely. They then struck
east, south of that river, and finally fell on it lower down—per-

DEVIL'S GATE, SWEETWATER RIVER, WYOMING.

faithful old Simon—I may say the whole trinity—played out on me.[17] About two hours before camping time the pack of one of my mules got so much out of order that I was obliged to stop to lash it again. Mr. Simon, who was in the habit of waiting for me on occasions of that kind, changed his notion and took it into his head to follow the party without me; the well-packed one followed suit, and it was all I could do to prevent the third one from leaving before getting his pack on; but as soon as that was done the gentleman took to his heels, and all three got into camp about an hour before me. The want of Simon was the cause of my being obliged to wade a small creek—tributary to the Sweetwater—which was very cold, although it was the 2d of July. I was wet up to my waist, and it was my guard late that night. When

haps via Whiskey [or Muddy] Gap, between the Green and the Seminole Mountains." It is due to Capt. H. M. Chittenden to say that this modification of my view resulted from his criticism, during correspondence which we had upon the whole subject of the overland Astorian routes. Capt. Chittenden has lately favored me with the blue print of a map on which he locates the main winter camp of the incoming Astorians in the bend of the N. Platte at Poison Spider creek, a little above Casper, Wyo.

Larpenteur's Journ. states that his party ascended the Sweetwater for six days, and that "on the second of July we arived on the Divide where we encamped."

[17] His riding-mule and two pack-mules composed the "whole trinity." Perhaps he forgot to put on the blinders!

I was wakened to go on guard my clothes were still
wet, and on that morning, the 3d of July, water
froze in our kettles nearly a quarter of an inch thick.
I felt quite chilly and was sick for about eight days.

As near as I can remember we reached the rendezvous on Green river on the 8th of July.[18]   There

[18] Orig. Journ. has: "On the fifth [of July] we arived to the
randezvous which was on the ques qui di river near Mr. Barna-
villes Fort which is supposed [writing in 1834] to have been
distroyed by the Black Feet."   The author's "Quesquidi" is
Green river, the principal fork of the Colorado; the Crow Indian
name has uncounted variants in spelling, among which I have
noticed Siskadee, Siskede-azzeah, Sheetskadee, and Seedskedee-
agie; the word is said to mean Prairie-hen river (with reference
to the sage grouse, *Centrocercus urophasianus*).   Our name,
Green river, translates Rio Verde of the Spanish, who came to it
somewhere about 1818, and were struck with the color of its
water.   Green river is also often and not improperly called the
Colorado, as it is the main upper reach of that great stream.
From South Pass it was two or three days' journey on the regular road S. W., down the Little and Big Sandy, to the rendezvous
on Green river, near Capt. Bonneville's post.   The exact location of this rendezvous, which Larpenteur does not give, is
recoverable from Irving's chaps. xix and xx, where it appears
that Bonneville, who had wintered 1832-33 elsewhere in the
mountains, reached Green river July 13, 1833, and "sent out
spies to his place of rendezvous on Horse creek," a small tributary
of the Green from the W.   "About four miles from the rendezvous
of Captain Bonneville was that of the American Fur Company
hard by which was that also of the Rocky Mountain Fur Company"—the latter being, of course, that to which Larpenteur
belonged.   This does not mean that the rendezvous where the
parties met was at Horse creek, for this creek is much higher

were still some of Capt. Bonneville's men in a small stockade. He had come up the year previous [1832]. Thus ended our journey so far.

up the Green, and was Bonneville's own place of rendezvous, to which he sent spies from the point where he met the other traders. The regular road passed W. from this vicinity by way of Black's and Ham's forks, and so on over to Bear river.

When the Wyeth expedition was at the rendezvous the following year (June 19–30, 1834), Townsend states in his Narr., 1839, p. 75, that he met there Wm. Sublette, Capts. Serre, Fitzpatrick, and other leaders. With him was the distinguished botanist, Thomas Nuttall; and "we were joined at the rendezvous by a Captain Stewart, an English gentleman of noble family, who is travelling for amusement, and in search of adventure. He has already been a year in the mountains," etc. This is the Englishman whom Larpenteur has named as accompanying his party in 1833. "Another Englishman," continues Townsend, p. 79, "a young man named Ashworth, also attached himself to our party." I am particular to cite Townsend in this connection, because his testimony is conclusive that the rendezvous was *not* on Horse creek. For example, he says, p. 69: "We left the Sweet-water, and proceeded in a *south-westerly* direction to Sandy river;" and again, p. 71: "Our course was still *down the Sandy river*," etc. Thus he reaches the rendezvous by the regular road which I have mentioned above, and it was where I have said. Nobody went up to that Horse creek place to pass from Green to Bear river,

CHAPTER III.

(1833.)

FROM GREEN RIVER RENDEZVOUS BY THE BIGHORN AND THE YELLOWSTONE TO THE MISSOURI.

THE day after we reached the rendezvous Mr. Campbell, with ten men, started to raise a beaver cache at a place called by the French Trou à Pierre, which means Peter's Hole.[1] As I was sick, Mr. Campbell left me in camp, and placed Mr. Fitzpatrick in

[1] I have not elsewhere found Trou à Pierre translated "Peter's" Hole—always Pierre or Pierre's Hole, the name it still bears. It is said to have been so called after one Pierre, an Iroquois in the employ of the H. B. Co., "who fell by the hands of the Blackfeet and gave his name to the fated valley of Pierre's Hole," says Irving's Bonneville, chap. x., date not given, stated to be "many" years before 1832. The history of the place dates back to 1811, when the outgoing overland Astorians passed through it, between Oct. 4 and 8; but it was then nameless. This party were en route from the main or S. fork of Snake river, at the mouth of Hoback's river, to the point on Henry's or N. fork of Snake river where Andrew Henry had established his post in 1810, and been driven therefrom in 1811. Their way was over the Teton range by Teton Pass into Pierre's Hole, which is the recess between the mountains just said and the Snake River range; the Hole is watered by the numerous affluents of Teton

charge during his absence, telling the latter to take good care of me, and if the man Redman, whom he left as clerk, did not answer, to try me. In a short time a tent was rigged up into a kind of saloon, and such drinking, yelling, and shooting as went on I, of course, never had heard before. Mr. Redman, among the rest, finally got so drunk that Mr. Fitzpatrick could do nothing with him, and there was not a sober man to be found in camp but myself. So Mr. Fitzpatrick asked me if I would try my hand at clerking. I remarked that I was willing to do my best, and at it I went. For several days nothing but whisky was sold, at $5 a pint. There were great quarrels and

river, from all the mountains round about, and the Teton flows into Henry's fork in the vicinity of the place where Henry's fort stood, but lower down. This post was on the left bank of Henry's fork, about opposite present Elgin, 2–3 m. from present Wilford, say 10 m. below confluence of Fall river with the main stream. Pierre's Hole was retraversed by the incoming Astorians early in October of the following year, 1812, and in Larpenteur's time had become a great resort. "Pierre's Hole" will be found marked on various maps, but the name seems to be lapsing of late years, like that of Pierre's river for the Teton. The meridian line between Wyoming and Idaho runs through Pierre's Hole, near long. 111° W.

The most notable event in the early history of Pierre's Hole is the fight with the Blackfeet of 1832, best narrated in Irving's chap. vi. A recent letter from John Ball, dated Grand Rapids, Mich., Oct. 14, 1874, published in Cont. Mont. Hist. Soc., i, 1876, pp. 111, 112, gives another notice of the same place in 1832: "I crossed the Rocky Mountains in 1832, in the party of Mr. Nathan-

fights outside, but I must say the men were very civil
to me.　Mr. Fitzpatrick was delighted, and wondered
to me why Mr. Campbell had not mentioned me for
'clerk in the first instance instead of that drunken Redman.　After seven or eight days Mr. Campbell returned with ten packs of beaver.　A few days afterward the rumor was circulated in camp that he was
about to sell out their interest in the mountains to
Fitzpatrick, Edmund Christy, Frap, and Gervais.
In the meantime sprees abated, and the trappers commenced to buy their little outfits, consisting of
blankets, scarlet shirts, tobacco, and some few
trinkets to trade with the Snake Indians, during
which transactions I officiated as clerk.

ie) Wyeth. . . In upper Missouri our party joined a trading
company headed by Mr. William Sublette, with whom we
traveled. A Mr. Robert Campbell of St. Louis was also of the
caravan. We passed Captain Bonneville's party, which was
traveling with wagons, between the Kansas and the Platte, went
up the North Platte and Sweetwater, and reached the South Pass
early in July. We kept close under the Wind River Mountains
for a hundred miles, and came to a branch of the Lewis river
(Snake river), and at Pierre's Hole, which was a famous resort,
met Sublette's trappers and the Flathead and Nez Perce Indians."
The reader will remember that this was the time and place of
Sublette's wounding, already mentioned by Larpenteur, p. 8.

The Orig. Journ. states that the party which went to "raize
the cash" in Pierre's Hole left July 5, and consisted of 18 men,
who returned July 15; two days after which camp was shifted a
little further down Green river, where there was better pastur-
age, and remained there until July 24.

The rumors at last became verified; the sales were effected, but things went on as usual until Mr. Campbell sent for me one morning. On entering his tent I was presented with a good cup of coffee and a large-sized biscuit; this was a great treat, for I believe that it was the first coffee I had drunk since I left Lexington. Then he remarked, " Charles, I suppose you have heard that I sold out our interest in the mountains; but I have reserved all your mess, ten mules, and the cattle (we had four cows and two bulls, intended for the Yellowstone). I have 30 packs of beaver, which Fitz is to assist me with as far as the Bighorn river, where I intend to make skin boats and take my beaver down to the mouth of the Yellowstone. There I expect to meet Sublette, who is to take the packs on to St. Louis. You are one of the ten men whom I have reserved, but Fitz would like much to have you remain with him, and I leave you the choice, to stay with him or come with me." My reply was, " Mr. Campbell, I have engaged to you, you have treated me like a gentleman, and I wish to follow you wherever you go." Upon which he said, " Very well, very well," with a kind smile; " go to your mess." On returning, my messmates, expecting some news, asked me what was the result of my visit to the boss; and, on being informed, a great shout of joy was the answer.

The beaver was all packed and pressed ready for the march; so the next day the order came to catch up the animals, receive our packs, and move camp. This was not our final departure; it was merely to get a fresh grazing ground for the mules and horses.

A day or so later we learned that a mad wolf had got into Mr. Fontenelle's camp about five miles from us, and had bitten some of his men and horses. My messmates, who were old hands, had heard of the like before, when men had gone mad. It was very warm, toward the latter end of July; we were in the habit of sleeping in the open air, and never took the trouble to put up the tent, except in bad weather; but when evening came the boys set up the tent. Some of the other messes asked, "What is that for?" The reply was, "Oh, mad wolf come—he bite me." When the time came to retire the pack saddles were brought up to barricade the entrance of our tent, the only one up in camp, excepting that of the boss. After all hands had retired nothing was heard in the camp except, now and then, the cry of "All's well," and some loud snoring, till the sudden cry of, "Oh, I'm bitten!"—then immediately another, and another. Three of our men were bitten that night,[2] all of them

<hr />

[2] This affair of the mad wolves is also narrated by Irving in Bonneville's Adventures, chap. xx; where, after describing the wild revelry and deviltry that went on in the several camps of

in the face. One poor fellow, by the name of George Holmes, was badly bitten on the right ear and face. All hands got up with their guns in pursuit of the animal, but he made his escape. When daylight came men were mounted to go in search, but nothing could be seen of him. It was then thought that he had gone and was not likely to return, and no further precaution was taken than the night before. But it seems that Mr. Wolf, who was thought far away, had hidden near camp; for about midnight the cry of " mad wolf " was heard again. This time the animal was among the cattle and bit our largest bull, which went mad afterward on the Bighorn, where we made the boats. The wolf could have been shot,[3] but orders were not to shoot in camp, for fear of accidentally killing some one, and so Mr. Wolf again escaped.

this great rendezvous, he says : " During this season of folly and frolic, there was an alarm of mad wolves in the two lower camps," *i. e.*, of the A. F. Co. and R. Mt. Co. The chapter ends with " another instance we have from a different person who was present in the encampment. One of the men of the Rocky Mountain Fur Company had been bitten," etc. This case seems to be no other than that of George Holmes, and very likely Larpenteur was Irving's informant.

[3] Larpenteur says in his Orig. Journ. that he could have shot the wolf, " but I was hindered by Captain Stward which was officer of guard at the time." He forgets to state, among events at the rendezvous, that on July 22 Mr. Gervais started with 30 men to trap in the " root diger's country, " *i. e.*, among the Digger Indians.

But we learned afterward that he had been killed by some of Mr. Fontenelle's men.

As well as I can remember it was the first week in August [*] when we were ordered to take final leave for the Horn. Our party was then much reduced; the members of the new company remained on Green river with the intention, according to custom, to set out through the mountains so soon as trapping time

[*] Orig. Journ. gives July 24 as date of final departure from the rendezvous for the Bighorn. That this is correct is shown by Irving's Bonneville, opening of chap. xxiii, where we read : "On the 25th of July [1833] Captain Bonneville struck his tents, and set out on his route for the Bighorn, . . . and soon fell upon the track of Mr. Robert Campbell's party, which had preceded him by a day." Irving's whole chapter, in fact, should be read with the present chapter of Larpenteur, as it gives many additional particulars. The two parties came together Aug. 4 : on which date Irving mentions Fitzpatrick, as well as Campbell : the English Captain Stewart (or Stuart), whom Larpenteur has dropped, though this guest was still with the party; and Nathaniel J. Wyeth, who was attached to Larpenteur's party, on his return from his outgoing of 1832 with Wm. Sublette and R. Campbell, after he had been to the Columbia and returning had met Bonneville at the rendezvous on Green river. The various parties continued together about a fortnight, before they separated on their several diverse routes. Bonneville set out for a rendezvous at Medicine Lodge on Aug. 17. Captain Stuart started for the Crows on his adventures, of which he had plenty, as we may read in Beckwourth's book. Wyeth went on ahead of Larpenteur's party, down the Bighorn in a bull-boat ; left Fort Cass Aug. 18, and reached Fort Union Aug. 24 ; Milton Sublette was with him. Irving's chap. xli traces Wyeth's journey.

commenced. Fitzpatrick came with us, with about
20 of his men; Harrison was with Fitz, intending to
winter in the mountains. We turned back on the
same route by which we had reached the rendezvous,
to Sweetwater, from which we struck off for Wind
river.[6] Two days after leaving the Sweetwater we

[6] The main upper reach of the Bighorn itself is so called above
the confluence of Popo-agie river. Wind river runs S. E. to this
confluence, whence the course of the Bighorn is almost N. to the
Yellowstone. Larpenteur retraversed South Pass and thus got
on the Sweetwater, but did not go far down the latter before
turning away from it—certainly nowhere near "Rock Independ-
ent," as he says by mistake in a passage above which I have
stricken out, as nothing of the sort is indicated by the Orig.
Journ. "Wind River" occurs in Irving's Astoria, orig. ed. 1836,
but the name is much older. The stream was first ascended by
the outgoing overland Astorians under Wilson Price Hunt, Sept.
9–14, 1811 ; and appears to have soon become known by its present name, though this does not occur in any Lewis and Clark
text, orig. ed. 1814. The Bighorn was of course so named from
the mountain sheep, *Ovis montana :* an Indian name of this animal is rendered ahsahta by Irving, and Arsata appears as an
alternative name of the river on Lewis' earliest map. In one place
in chap. xxiv "Big Horse" runs through all the eds. of Astoria
by misprint. In David Thompson's MS. I found the name
"River of Large Corn," evidently mistranslating the French
Grosse Corne (big horn). Pappah-ahje of the above text is one
of many variants of the Crow Indian name now usually rendered
Popo-agie, meaning Reed river. Bonneville spells it Po-po-az-
ze-ah. In his Bonneville Irving mistakenly translates it "Head"
river. On consulting Dr. Matthews in this case, I am favored
with the following : "Popo-Agie is a Crow name. As you know,
Crow and Hidatsa are closely allied tongues, and as you know

reached Wind river, near the mouth of a small stream called Pappah-ah-je, which place Dr. Harrison visited on account of the remarkable oil spring which puts into that stream. Some distance from the river we learned by one of the men, who had gone ahead to find a good encampment, that the Indians, the night previous, had shot a trapper asleep through the ear, that the ball had come out under his jaw, and that he had an arrow-point in his shoulder-blade. Three old trappers [6] had left Green river some time before us, intending to meet us on Wind river. Dr. Harrison extracted the arrow-point and dressed the wound, which he pronounced not dangerous. We remained in camp two days. From this point until we got to the other side of the mountains, game became so scarce that we had to live for two days on such berries and roots as we could find. Two days before reach-

also, the sounds of *o* and *u* are easily interchanged in any language, English included. Now look at my Hidatsa Dictionary for the words *púpu* and *dzi* (ahzhee), and put them together; then look at the word for head (*atu*) and see if you can make "Head River" out of this name. *Púpu* is, I believe, the common reed, *Phragmites communis*. This plant figures again in the Tobacco Garden story, which comes later on in Larpenteur."

[6] These were three of Mr. Frapp's men. A fuller account of the shooting is given in the Orig. Journ., from which it appears that the Indians were Shoshones who, disguised with bushes on their heads, crept up so close to their victim that the powder burned his cap. Irving's chap. xxiii notes the same incident.

ing the Horn one of our bulls commenced to show some symptoms of hydrophobia by bellowing at a great rate, and pawing the ground. This scared my poor friend Holmes, who was still in our party, but not destined to reach the Yellowstone. He was a young man from New York, well educated, and we became quite attached to each other on our long journey. The poor fellow now and then asked me if I thought he would go mad; although thinking within myself he would, being so badly bitten, I did all I could to make him believe otherwise. When he said to me, " Larpenteur, don't you hear the bull—he is going mad—I am getting scared," I do believe I felt worse than he did, and scarcely knew how to answer him. The bull died two days after we arrived at the Horn, and I learned, some time afterward, from Mr. Fontenelle, that Holmes had gone mad. For some days he could not bear to cross the small streams which they struck from time to time, so that they had to cover him over with a blanket to get him across; and at last they had to leave him with two men until his fit should be over. But the men soon left him and came to camp. Mr. Fontenelle immediately sent back after him; but when they arrived at the place, they found only his clothes, which he had torn off his back. He had run away quite naked, and never was found. This ended my poor friend Holmes.

It was about the 10th of August when we reached the Horn, which is the same as Wind river, only the latter loses its name after crossing the mountains. It is not navigable through the mountains, I am informed, even for a small canoe; and this is the reason why our boats had to be made on this side of the mountain. So, immediately after our arrival, a large party of hunters, with men and mules, started out, with the view of bringing in hides rather than meat; but, as luck would have it, Mr. Vasquez, clerk and old mountain man, killed one of the fattest buffalo I ever saw. Three days after this three boats were completed,[7] and everything in readiness to leave. In the morning I was sent for by Mr. Campbell, who then gave me some instructions I was not expecting. "Now," said he, "Charles, I am going down by the river with my beaver. Mr. Vasquez will go down by land in charge of the party, with the mules and cattle. There will be but five of you. You are going to travel through the most dangerous part of the country. Mr. Vasquez will keep ahead of the party on the strict lookout, and should anything happen to him, I wish you to take charge of the party." My reply was, "Very well, sir," though such instructions, I must confess, made me feel a little nervous. But it did not last; I very soon became quite cheerful, and

[7] The bull-boats were made about Aug. 12-15, by Orig. Journ.

anxious to be under way. Mr. Campbell started that same day, and we all left early next morning. For the four first days we traveled slowly and quietly. We could not travel fast on account of the cattle, whose feet were badly worn out and tender. On the fifth morning,[8] a little while after we left camp, we saw Mr. Vasquez coming back toward us, which made us suspect he had discovered something; we thought it might have been a band of buffalo. But when he came up to us he said that he had discovered Indians—three, on the other side of the river; but he was sure we had not been discovered by them, and moved that we should go near the river, to secure water and make some kind of a fort, for defense in case of attack. As he was in charge, and an old experienced man, we readily consented. So on we went to the river, but on arrival we found, to our great surprise, the opposite shore red with Indians, who commenced to yell enough to frighten Old Nick himself. No time to make a fort, or even to un-saddle, before they began to throw themselves into the river and make toward us. Mr. Vasquez ordered us to take position behind a large cluster of cotton-woods and cock our rifles, but not to shoot until he gave the order. So there we stood in readiness, like

[8] Aug. 17 is this date by Orig. Journ., which says it was after two days' travel that the incident occurred.

veterans; the first fright was over, and we were ready to make the Indians pay dearly for our hair. None of us understanding their language, we made sure they were Blackfeet, and fight we must. In less time than it takes me to write this, they were upon us. One tall scoundrel came up a little ahead of the rest with a white flag, making signs not to shoot. An old French mountaineer named Paulette Desjardins understood a few words of Crow, and as the Indian pronounced the name of his tribe, the old man said "They are Crows *—there is no danger for our lives, but they are great thieves." Mr. Vasquez also knew as much about them as the old man did, and so we let them come up. Then the shaking of hands took place, and our hearts went back into the right place again. As we had a large supply of buffalo meat, we made a feast, which they appeared to relish very much, and then they expressed a desire to open trade; but we had no goods for that purpose.

We had not gone more than three miles when we discovered some ten Indians galloping toward us as fast as their horses could go; we stopped until they approached us, when we found that they were the chiefs and leading men of the camp. They looked splendid,

* "They made us sign that they were Ab-sah-rokier-bats-ats meaning they were the great crow Indians." Orig. Journ. Literally, "we are Crow men:" see Matthews, Hidatsa Gram., paragraphs 33, 168.

dressed in the best of Indian costumes, and mounted on fat ponies. They all shook hands and made signs that they would look for a good place to camp, and for us to follow. Somewhat against our will we did so. It was not long before the desired spot was found, and the whole camp soon made its appearance, containing upward of 400 lodges. This was a great sight for me, who had never seen such a formidable Indian camp. The Crows, at that time, generally roamed together, and on this particular occasion they looked richer than any other Indians, for they had just made their trade at the fort, one day's march from where we were. The Crows did not drink then, and for many years remained sober; it was not until a few years ago, when they were driven out of their country by the Sioux, and became a part of the tribe on the Missouri, that they took to drinking with the Assiniboines. As they did not drink, their trade was all in substantial goods, which kept them always well dressed, and extremely rich in horses; so it was really a beautiful sight to see that tribe on the move. As soon as the proper place was found for encamping, the chief made us a sign to unsaddle and to put all our plunder in a circle which he himself described; and on the arrival of the camp his lodge was immediately erected over it, so that all was safe.

We finally left the Crow camp and soon reached

Fort Cass,[10] then in charge of Mr. Tulloch, who was a
man possessed of good common sense, very reliable,
and brave withal. He was called the Crane by all the
Indians, on account of the extreme length and slen-
derness for which he was remarkable—almost a curiosity; he was extremely popular among the Crows,
and well liked by the mountain men. When he left
Fort Union to establish this new post, Mr. [Kenneth]
McKenzie requested him to take all such articles as
the Crows might fetch, so as to get them in the way
of trade. His first returns consisted mostly of elk,
deer, and all kinds of horns, which made great mirth
at Fort Union; yet his trade had been profitable. It

[10] Fort Cass, on Yellowstone, 2 m. below the mouth of the Bighorn, was established in 1832 by A. J. Tullock—the same for
whom Tullock's fork of the Bighorn was named. He is frequently
Tulloch, and Tulleck occurs throughout Beckwourth's book, in
which much is said of the man and his post: see also L. and C.,
ed. 1893, p. 1152.

"In 1832, McKenzie sent Tullock, with forty men, to build a
fort at the mouth of the Big Horn river," says James Stuart, in
Cont. Mont. Hist. Soc., i. 1876, p. 88. This is right; but his
further statements require correction. "Tullock built the fort
named Van Buren, on the south side of the Yellowstone, about
three miles below the mouth of the Big Horn." But *this* was
Fort Cass. The writer goes on to say that in 1863 he saw the
location, marked by ashes and some standing chimneys. In so
stating he means not Cass but Van Buren, which was burned by
Larpenteur himself, in 1842, as we shall see in due course; and
Van Buren stood at the mouth of the Rosebud, not near the Big-

was started again, and when we arrived there it was
his second year. We learned that this was a very
dangerous post; they had had some men killed by the
Blackfeet, and were even afraid to go out to chop
wood. This fort was situated about two miles below
the mouth of the Horn.

Next day at ten o'clock we were again on the move,
with a journey of about 250 miles before us, to reach
the mouth of the Yellowstone. Nothing worthy of
note took place during this part of our journey, which
would have been extremely pleasant had it not been
for anticipated danger from Indians. We had to
erect a large pen for our animals every night, for fear

horn. The writer follows with other statements, singularly
wrong. Speaking of the Crows as an insolent, treacherous
tribe, he says: "They wanted the location of their trading-post
changed nearly every year, consequently they had four trading
posts built from 1832 to 1850, viz.: Ft. Cass, built by Tullock, on
the Yellowstone, below Van Buren [*read* below the Bighorn], in
1836 [*read* 1832]; Ft. Alexander, built by Lawender [*read* Lar-
penteur], still lower down on the Yellowstone river, in 1848
[*read* 1842], and Ft. Sarpey [*read* Sarpy] built by Alexander
Culbertson, in 1850, at the mouth of the Rosebud." Mr.
Stuart was a well-informed and usually accurate man; this
passage is so far wrong that I am inclined to think that his
copy got mixed in the type-setting. Certainly no reader who
did not know who built Fort Alexander at Adams prarie in 1842
would guess that "Lawender" stood for Larpenteur. The date
of founding of Fort Van Buren is 1835; it lasted eight years. Fort
Sarpy, named for John B.. lasted six years, 1850–55.

of sudden attacks, and to stand frequent guard, as our party was small.   But we lived on the fat of the land, as at that season game was in good order, and the Yellowstone valley abounded with all kind of game at that early period, and for many subsequent years.   We were often frightened at large bands of elk, which, at a distance, bear the exact appearance of a mounted party of Indians, till, by the aid of a good spyglass, our fears were relieved.   Our two cows added a great deal to our good living; as we had no coffee, milk was a great relish.   We made but slow progress, on account of the cattle, whose feet became very tender, and finally got so bad that we were obliged to make shoes of raw buffalo hide.

We arrived safe and sound at the mouth of the Yellowstone on the 3d of September,[11] and thus ended our long trip.   We were soon discovered by our people, who were at the landing where our fort was to be erected, two miles below the mouth of the Yellowstone, and were informed that Mr. William

[11] Orig. Journ. happily agrees to this date—Sept. 3, 1833—perhaps the first absolute identity between itself and the present text thus far.   It appears that the party went down the S. side or right bank of the Yellowstone, as it speaks of crossing Tongue and Rosebud rivers ; two or three days after passing which latter the Yellowstone was crossed and the journey completed on its other side.   The Journ. has : "On the third of September on our arrival at this place we saw a paper stuck on a pole stating

Sublette arrived there eight days before and Mr.
Campbell three; but he had capsized in the Horn, lost
two packs of beaver, and been near losing his life.
Otherwise everything was right; they would have
been glad to see us across, but it was too late in the
evening to attempt this, as we had to swim. Now
that I am obliged to pass a night on this side, if my
reader will be so kind as to help me we will try to
find out how long I have been in the saddle. As
near as I can come, it is five months lacking four
days.[12] We should have been much better pleased if
we could have crossed over on our arrival; still we
felt quite merry, and it was a long time before we
could go to sleep.

In the evening, after we caught up our stock, one
could hear great talk to the mules, calling them by
name, telling them that they were near the end of
their journey, and what they might expect in future;
it was really amusing, and it was almost thought that
the poor dumb beasts understood what was said to

Mr. Sublette's arrivel and [that he] was at the time two miles
below the mouth [of the Yellowstone] on the north side of the
Missouri where he intended to build his fort which is two miles
and a half from fort Union belonging to the American fur Company: and our fort was named fort William after the name of
the owner whos name was William Sublette."

[12] By our text ostensibly Apr. 7–Sept. 3, agreeing within a week
with the Orig. Journ. See note [16], p. 12.

them. All hands were up early, mules and cattle
turned out, and we waited impatiently to cross over.
Between 10 and 11 a. m. Mr. Johnesse, who had come
down by water with Mr. Campbell, and was still our
foreman, appeared on the opposite shore to show us
the place where we had to swim the stock across.
The river at that season was low, and the channel so
narrow that we could plainly hear all he said. When
we got ready to drive the stock in, he hallooed to
me, thinking I did not know how to swim, to take
hold of the bull's tail. Not being an expert in the
science, I took his advice and the bull's tail too, and,
making use of my three loose limbs, I reached the
opposite shore with ease. In a short time we were
all safe on the north bank of the Missouri, upward of
2000 miles from St. Louis.[13]

[13] In round numbers, as then supposed, like all of Larpenteur's
estimates thus far. The channel mileage of the Missouri, from
its mouth to the Yellowstone, is now given as 1,760 m. St. Louis
is now 17 m. below the mouth of the Missouri.

From the utmost source of the Missouri, above Upper Red Rock
lake, by so-called Red Rock, Beaverhead, and Jefferson rivers, to
Three Forks, is 398 m., thence to confluence of the Missouri with
the Mississippi, 2,547 ; thence by the Mississippi to the Gulf of
Mexico, 1,276 ; total channel mileage, 4,221—making the longest
continuous water-course in the world. See Brower, The Missouri,
1897, pp. 117-121.

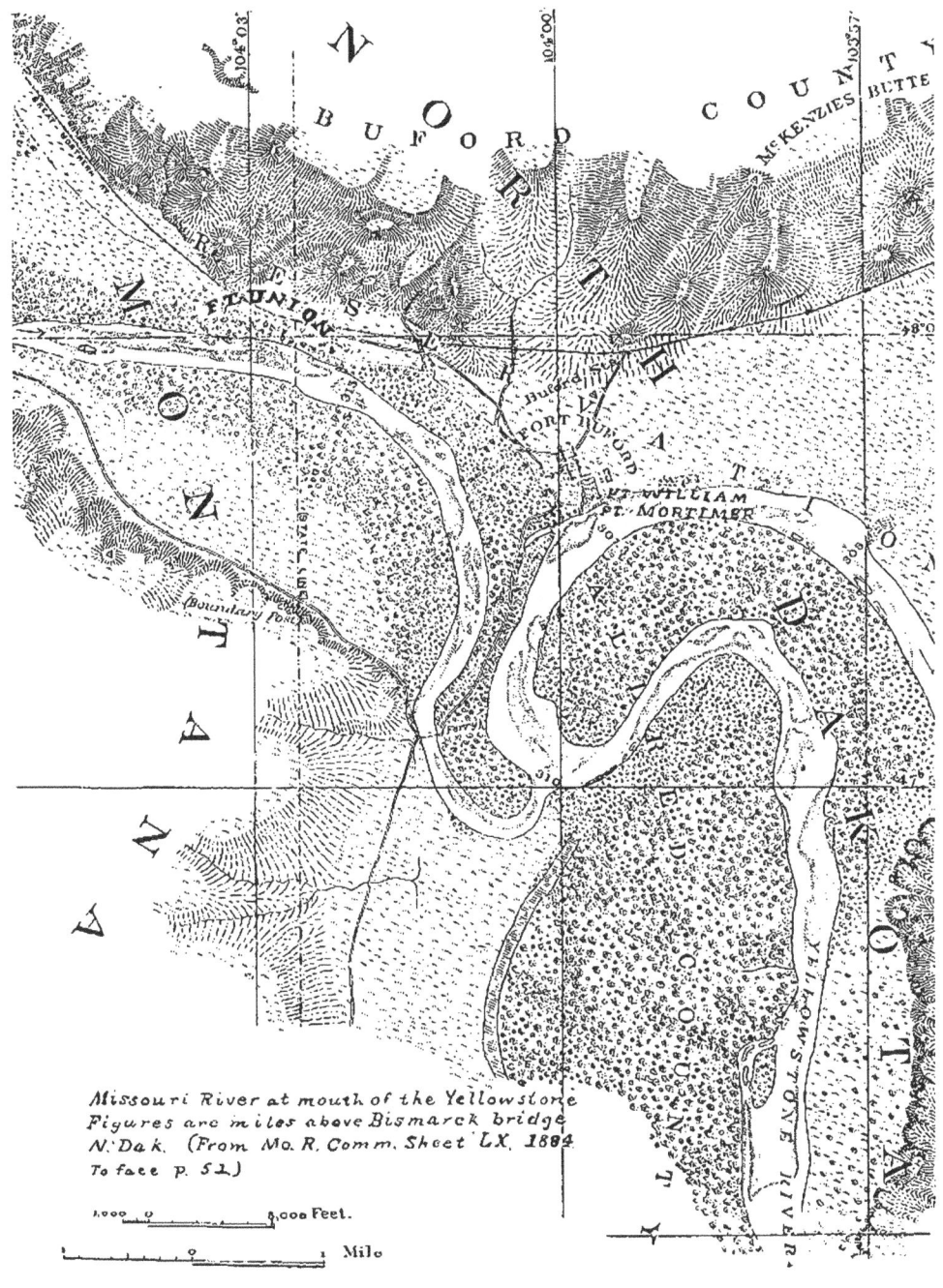

Missouri River at mouth of the Yellowstone
Figures are miles above Bismarck bridge
N. Dak. (From Mo. R. Comm. Sheet LX. 1884
To face p. 52)

CHAPTER IV.

(1833-34.)

FORT WILLIAM.

Soon after crossing the Missouri we were again in company with our former messmates, and some of our other acquaintances who had come down the Yellowstone by water; the meeting was indeed a cause for rejoicing. We were now altogether about 30 men, encamped in the willows on the river bank, about 300 yards from where Fort William [1] was to

[1] Here we have exact data concerning the establishment of Fort William in opposition to Fort Union of the A. F. Co. The latter stood on the left bank of the Missouri, about the same distance above the mouth of the Yellowstone that Fort William was below the same point, and owing to the loop of the Missouri into which the Yellowstone fell, the two posts were about as far from each other as either was from the Yellowstone. The site of Fort William was nearly identical with that of the subsequent (and present) military post, Fort Buford. This original wooden Fort William is the one mentioned, not by name, in Cont. Mont. Hist. Soc. i, 1876, p. 84, where it is said that " Robert Campbell and Sublette built a trading post where Fort Buford now stands, in 1833." Later on, another fort called William was built of adobes, on the same spot, or very close by, and the walls of this

be erected, and to be so called in honor of William Sublette. As we had no tents those willows sheltered us from the wind, and enabled us to make comfortable cabins. Next day operations commenced for building the fort; some men getting out pickets for the stockade, others sawing logs, etc. Seeing the necessity of having safer quarters, we went to work with all

one were still standing in 1865, when they were torn down to be used in building Buford.

The Orig. Journ. agrees to Nov. 15 as the date of moving into Fort William and beginning to trade buffalo robes, wolves, foxes, and beavers. The fort, as originally constructed of wood, is fully described in the text beyond.

At same date of Nov. 15, the Journal continues : "We were obliged to erect out Posts one was about fifty miles up the Missouri and the other about 80 miles up the Yellow Stone the former was managed by Mr. Antoine Jeanisse [read Jeunesse] and the latter by Mr. Wm Almond from virginia." The outpost "about 50 miles up the Missouri" was located at Frenchman's Point. Both this and the Yellowstone outpost were abandoned next year, 1834.

The name Fort William runs through travelers' and traders' writings from 1833 to 1866, when the last traces of any structure so called disappeared, as just said. But all mention of the adobe structure so called must be distinguished from any reference to the original wooden Fort William, which only endured about a year, when it was eradicated, and its material taken up to Union. The name stuck to the *place*, and was bestowed upon an adobe structure which was in evidence on the spot to 1866 ; but the date of erection of this building has escaped my search. In 1843 the Opposition post, on or very near the original site of Fort William, was called Fort Mortimer ; Larpenteur says so

our might every day, and Sunday too; and by the 15th of November got into our comfortable quarters, after which the Sunday work was stopped. The day we moved in was a holiday, and in the evening a great feast was given us by Mr. Campbell—Mr. Sublette having left in the keel boat a few days after our arrival, taking with him about ten men. It consisted

expressly, beyond; and Audubon's Journal of that year repeatedly speaks of Fort Mortimer (vol. ii. 1897, *passim*, from p. 31 to p. 148), but has no Fort William. Boller says, in his Among the Indians, 1868, p. 42, that one afternoon in 1858, "we came in sight of Fort William, three miles below the mouth of the Yellowstone, where we landed"; and again, p. 46: " A short stay [at Fort Union] and we were off again, passing the mouth of the Yellowstone to Fort William, where a huge beacon fire was blazing on the bank, surrounded by a group of wild-looking mountaineers, eagerly awaiting our return. Morning at length dawned upon the dismantled fort, where but a short time before all had been life and animation. It had now a deserted and forlorn appearance, and in a little while the crumbling adobe walls would be all that remained of what had once been a bustling post. We took on board the proceeds of the last year's trade," etc. From this it would appear that a post known as Fort William was operative to 1857-58, and that this year was the last of it. In 1863, when Boller was again at Fort Union, he says, p. 369: " of old Fort William nothing was standing save a chimney or two, and portions of the crumbling adobe walls ;" and p. 372: " The ruins of Fort William were in plain sight [from Union] and the mountaineers spoke regretfully of the good old times when both Posts were in the full tide of success, and of the hospitalities that were so freely exchanged between them when the trading season was over."

of half a pint of flour to each man, one cup of coffee, one of sugar, and one of molasses, to four men. Out of this a becoming feast was made, consisting of thick pancakes, the batter containing no other ingredient than pure Missouri water, greased with buffalo tallow; but as I had had nothing of the kind for upward of six months, I thought I had never tasted anything so good in my life, and swore I would have plenty of the like if I ever got back to the States.

After this our work was changed in some respects. I was appointed carter, as I was not a very good hand with an ax, and soon equipped with an old cart [2] purchased from some of the half-breeds, who had come over early in the fall, and an American horse, which had been brought to this place by Paulette Desjardins, who had come with us as a freeman, but had sold his small outfit to Mr. Campbell and engaged in the capacity of cook. This horse was an old, overgrown, broken-winded beast, which would groan tremendously on starting his load, and keep it up for about a

[2] This was a one-horse, two-wheeled cart built of wood without any iron whatever, the ramshackle affair being held together with rawhide. But the "Red River cart," as it was called because it was made in this fashion by the Canadian French and their half-breeds of the Red River of the North, answered all ordinary purposes, and many thousands of these primitive vehicles were in use during the years of which Larpenteur writes, especially on the annual buffalo hunts which were conducted on the plains in large companies.

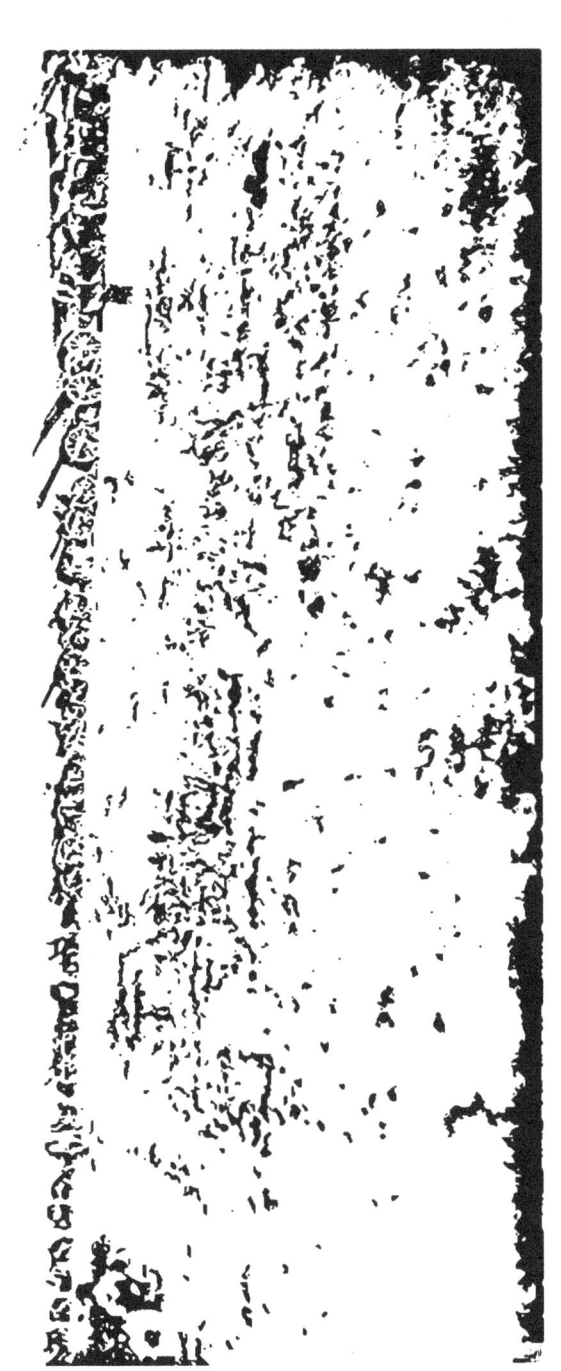

CAMP OF PEMBINA HALF BREEDS, WITH THEIR "RED RIVER CARTS."

hundred yards afterward, at which I could not help laughing. Here I am, a regular carter of Fort William, dressed in cowskin pants, cowskin coat, buckskin shirt, wolfskin cap, red flannel undershirt, and a blue check shirt over that, stepping along behind my old horse and cart. This great suit was intended to last my time out, under faithful promise, made to myself, to leave the country as soon as my engagement should be up; for I began to find that I was in a bad box. There had been some trading previous to our entering the fort, but none of importance except one, which took place about two weeks after, as I will now relate.[3]

[3] A long biographical sketch of Tchatka or Gaucher, otherwise Left Hand, the renowned Assiniboine chief, occupies Letter xiii, pp. 168–205, of De Smet's Western Missions and Missionaries, New York, 1859. "He was a crafty, cruel, deceitful man, a bad Indian, in every sense of the word ; his life was full of horrors." He seems to have been particularly infamous as a secret poisoner, and his arts as such, together with his theological juggleries, made him the most feared and best obeyed man of the tribe he led for some forty years. This great perverted genius died at Fort Union in the autumn of 1843, soon after a crushing defeat of his band by the Arikaras, from whom he had fled ignominiously. Among his names or titles, besides Gauché or Gaucher, which De Smet translates Awkward, are Wakontonga or Great Medicine ; Mina-Yougha or Knife-holder ; and Tatokanan or the Kid. De Smet's story is no doubt substantially correct, as he received it from Mr. Denig, "and from a worthy Canadian interpreter." Both of these men resided many years among the Assiniboines, knew Tchatka well, and witnessed many of his acts.

The news came by an Indian that Gauché, the great chief of the Assiniboines and the terror of all the neighboring tribes, was coming in to trade with about 200 buffalo robes, beside many small peltries. As Mr. Campbell had not yet been able to turn any of the chiefs from the American Fur Company's Fort Union, Gauché was not expected to come to us. But as he was a queer kind of a grizzly-bear fellow, very odd in his way, Mr. Campbell thought he might try his luck with Gauché; so he sent his interpreter and me along to see what we could do—for I must remark that, although I was only a carter, I slept in the store and assisted in trade at night. This was the favorite time for the Indians, so that I frequently traded most of the night and went to my carting in the morning. When we reached the place where the Indians had stopped, as was the custom, to vermilion and dress themselves before entering Fort Union, where their reception was awaited with the American flag up and the cannon loaded, ready for the salute, the interpreter of the Big Fort, as Fort Union was called, had already arrived on the spot. Shaking hands with the old man, he said: " Well, I hope you will not fork * to-day. The great chief of the big fort has sent me after you, and he is well prepared to

*That is, turn aside to go in another direction, as a road does when it forks.

receive you. I hope you will not make me ashamed by going with those one-winter-house traders." The old man was listening with half an intention [6]; and, as we approached him, looked the interpreter straight in the face and said: " If your great chief had sent any other but you I would have gone to him, but I don't go with the biggest liar in the country." Then he made a sign to his people to get on the move, crying out now and then, ", Co-han! Co-han!" which meant " Hurry up!" I found out afterward that this was a favorite expression of his. So, to the great astonishment of Mr. Campbell and all the others, we made our triumphant entrance into Fort William. We learned afterward that Mr. McKenzie was not at all surprised at the old fellow's caper, for he knew Gauché of old.

It was not until night that we all got ready to trade. It must be remembered that liquor, at that early day, was the principal and most profitable article of trade, although it was strictly prohibited by law, and all the boats on the Missouri were thoroughly searched on passing Fort Leavenworth.[6] Notwithstanding this, Mr. Sublette had managed to pass through what he

[6] Undecided in mind whether or not he would " fork," to trade at William instead of Union.

[6] An amusing instance of the way liquor was sometimes smuggled past Fort Leavenworth, with or without the connivance of

wanted for his trade all along the Missouri; but the American Fur Company, having at one time been detected and had their liquor confiscated, erected a distillery at Fort Union, and obtained their corn from the Gros Ventres and Mandans. I will say more, in future, about this distillery.

The liquor trade started at dark, and soon the singing and yelling commenced. The Indians were all locked up in the fort, for fear that some might go to Fort Union, which was but 2½ miles distant. Imagine the noise—upward of 500 Indians, with their squaws, all drunk as they could be, locked up in the small space. The old devil Gauché had provided himself with a pint tin cup, which I know he did not let go during the whole spree, and every now and then he would rush into the store with his cup, and it was " Co-han "—telling me to fill it—and " Co-han! hurry up about it, too! " This was a great night, but I wished that the old rascal and his band had gone to the big fort. At last daylight came and the spree abated; a great many had gone to sleep, and the goods trade did not commence until the afternoon; but old Co-han, with his cup, kept on the move pretty much of the time. It was not until midnight that

the officials whose duty it was to stop it, may be read in Audubon and his Journals, by Miss M. R. Audubon, New York, Scribner's Sons, 1897, i, p. 479).

the trade was entirely over, and early next morning they moved away, with the exception of the old man and a few of his staff of loafing beggars.

Mr. Campbell, who was anxious to secure Gauché for the winter, thought to make him a very impressive speech previous to his departure. So the old bear was invited into Mr. Campbell's room, and, after quite a lengthy speech, during which the old fellow made no reply, not even by a grunt, he merely said, " Are you a-going to give me some salt before I leave?" This being all the satisfaction Mr. Campbell received for his long speech, he could not refrain from laughing. The old devil got his salt, with some other small presents, and then departed without leaving any sign of his intention to return. Thus ended this trade.

Mr. Campbell happened to be out of luck this year, owing to the very warm fall of 1833, which kept the buffalo far north, and the winter trade of 1833-34 was a poor one; the Indians had no confidence in his remaining, so that the bulk of the trade went to the big American Company in spite of all we could do. Fortunately for us working hands, a small trade was done in the early part of the fall, or we should have fared much worse than we did—which was bad enough, as I will go on to explain. The jerked buffalo meat which had been traded from the Indians lasted but a little while, and after this our rations con-

sisted of about a pint of pounded meat, which had
been prepared and was brought in by the squaws.
This is what pemmican is made of; it has to be mixed
with grease to be eaten, but the tallow for this purpose we had to buy. This was sold at 50 cents per
bladder, in which it was put up by the squaws, and
which weighed from five to eight pounds. I had a
partner, a German, and we could together purchase
a bladder; but as to salt and pepper, which we had also
to buy—salt $1 a pint, pepper $2—we were not in
partnership; each had his small sack containing pepper and salt mixed, and used it as he thought proper.
This was all we could get—no sugar, no coffee—
nothing but cold water to wash the meat down.
This was generally given to us for our breakfast, then
lyed [1] corn for dinner and supper. This was pretty
good, but it went so hard on the salt and pepper that
I began to think that I scarcely earned my salt. This
kind of living lasted nearly all winter, with the exception of a deer or an elk which the hunters would now
and then kill near the fort; but, true to my word, I
entered no complaint.

I will here describe the construction of Fort William, which was after the usual formation of trading
posts. It was first erected precisely on the spot

[1] Corn soaked in lye to remove the hulls of the grains. See for
example my Henry and Thompson Journs., 1897, p. 248.

where the Fort Buford [8] sawmill now [about 1871] stands; but then it was about 200 yards farther from the river, the bank having caved in to that distance. It was 150 feet front and 130 deep. The stockade was of cottonwood logs, called pickets, 18 feet in length, hewn on three sides and planted three feet in the ground. The boss' house stood back, opposite the front door; it consisted of a double cabin, having two rooms of 18×20 feet, with a passage between them 12 feet wide. There was a store and warehouse 40 feet in length and 18 feet in width; two rooms for the men's quarters 16×18 feet, a carpenter's shop, blacksmith's shop, ice house, meat house, and two splendid bastions. The whole was completed by Christmas of 1833. The bastions were built more for amusement than for protection against hostile Indi-

[8] The establishment of Fort Buford was immediately followed by the downfall of Fort Union, and thus the mouth of the Yellowstone passed from commercial to military control. This was in 1866, when Buford started as a one-company post, increased to five companies in 1867 ; the military reservation of 30 square miles was announced in general orders No. 21, Headquarters of the Dept. of Dakota, dated July 16, 1868, and subsequently declared. Building went on for several years, and Buford was a great place when I was there in 1874 : I last saw it in 1893. During 1866–68, at least 14 soldiers and citizens were killed by Sioux at Buford or in its immediate vicinity ; an attack in force was made Aug. 20, 1868. A good description of the establishment, by Dr. J. P. Kimball, U. S. A., may be read in Circular No. 4, Surgeon General's Office, Washington, 1870, pp. 400–405.

ans; for, at that time, although they were constantly
at war with other tribes, there was not the least danger for any white men except the free trappers, and
we could go hunting in all directions with perfect
safety. Large war parties frequently came to the
fort, but behaved very well, taking their leave after
getting a few loads of ammunition and some tobacco.

This post was not the only one which was out of
luck, for all those along the Missouri proved a failure.
Sublette, being apprised of this, sold out during the
winter of 1833-34,[9] to the American Fur Company—
as I learned afterward, very much to the displeasure
of Mr. McKenzie, who wished to break us down com-

[9] The Orig. Journ. gives some incidents of the winter of 1833-
34, which the Autobiog. omits. These are in brief : On Jan. 15
1834, the Mr. Almond already mentioned as in charge of an
outpost was robbed by Indians and his life threatened ; he was
obliged to leave his place, where he had traded only 1½ pack of
robes, and a few packs of wolves. About the same time Mr.
" Jeannisse "was attacked by some half-breeds, who robbed him,
and he had a narrow escape for his life ; the half-breeds had been
hired by Mr. Campbell as interpreters for the Assiniboines and
Crees, but got in a drunken quarrel, with the result said. On
Mar. 20, 1834, Mr. J. returned to Fort William with 16 packs of
robes, and a few wolf- and fox-skins. Mr. Vasquez, who had
been sent to the Crows, traded 30 packs of robes and one pack of
beaver. At Fort William the trade was 100 packs of robes, 5 of
beaver, 6 of wolf, and one of fox and rabbit ; the opposition
(Fort Union, A. F. Co.) made 430 packs of robes; "as to other
peltries I was never informed, but I am sure it exceeded ours."

pletely, as a warning to any one who might oppose such a formidable and well-conducted company.

It was not until about the 10th of June, 1834, that an express arrived, informing us of the sale, and that the steamer would be up some time between that date and the 1st of July. This news was of little importance to me, as I had made up my mind to leave, and thought that nothing could induce me to remain in the country. In those days there was but one steamer a year up river this far, and great was always the rejoicement on its arrival. This was the Assiniboine;[10] the boat made her appearance on the 24th of June, having on board the gentlemen who were to take inventories of all the posts belonging to the American Fur Company, as old Mr.

[10] The Assiniboine was the boat which had brought up Maximilian, Prince of Wied, in 1833. She was a single-engine sidewheeler, owned by the A. F. Co.; John Carlisle, master; lost next year, June 1, 1835, by fire, at the head of Sibley island, near Little Heart river, in vicinity of present Bismarck, N. Dak. The boat had grounded when river was falling and was soon left high and dry. A lighter was to be built to float her cargo down to St. Louis, and the steamer was to be left till the river should rise ; but before she could be discharged she took fire from a stovepipe in the cabin, and was a total loss, including cargo, which consisted of 1,185 packs of robes and peltries, and a large collection of Indian curios, from the mouth of the Yellowstone. "There were four live buffaloes on board, which were run into the river and reached the shore by swimming." Chittenden, App. WW of Annual. Rep. Chf. Engrs., 1897, p. 3873.

Astor had this year sold out to Pierre Chouteau and Co.[11] A few days after the arrival of the steamer the transfer of goods and peltries took place.   Of the latter there were very few—70 packs of robes, 10 in a pack, which made 700 robes; 16 packs of wolves, 30 to the pack; and some few red and gray foxes.

In the meantime preparations were made for depar ture, which was to be in a large Mackinaw boat. While these were going on my occupation was that of horse guard. The idea of returning to the States was indeed very pleasant; while lying on the grass the thought of relating to Baltimore friends my mountain stories would make me feel, as the Indian says, " Big man me."   Best of all, I had the means to accomplish my journey; for, out of my wages of $296 I had saved over $200, thanks to not indulging too much in pancake parties.   Coffee being $1 a pint, sugar $1, and flour 25 cents, many of my poor comrades came out in debt.

One fine day [July 2, 1834] I was sent for by Mr. Campbell—I could not imagine what for.   I had not

[11] " In 1834. Mr. Astor, being advanced in years, sold out the stock of the company, and transferred the charter to Ramsey Crooks and his associates," Kelton, Ann. Mackinac, Whitney ed., 1886, p. 74.   " In 1834, Astor sold his interests to Chouteau, Valle and Company, of St. Louis, and retired from the business," Chittenden, The Yellstn., 1895, p. 35. confirmed by Larpenteur.   Mr. Astor d. Mar. 29, 1848 ; Mr. Crooks, June 6, 1859, in New York, in his 73d year.

yet shed my winter garments, which had become by this time quite greasy; and had it not been for my blue check shirt, which happened to be clean at the time, I should have been taken for a very dirty man. Imagine my surprise, on entering Mr. Campbell's room, to find myself in the presence of Mr. McKenzie, who was at that time considered the king of the Missouri; and, from the style in which he was dressed, I thought really he was a king. Without any introduction he immediately asked me if I would engage to him. Having made my plans to go home and not knowing but what he wanted me for a common hand, my reply was a short " No, sir," after which I made for the door and returned to my duty. The same evening, after I had brought in the horses, Mr. Campbell sent for me again, and then said: " Charles, I omitted to inform you of the conversation I had yesterday about you with Mr. McKenzie. This was the cause of his coming to-day. He did not want to engage you as a common hand; he wanted you for a clerk, and I should advise you to see him. He is very much of a gentleman, and I think you will do well. You will act as you think proper—but this is my advice." Then I had to combat my made-up plans, and give up all idea of returning to Baltimore. This I thought I could never do. I did not sleep much that night.

Next morning, while I was not feeling disposed
to see Mr. McKenzie, Mr. Campbell said, " Well,
Charles, are you going to try your luck?" My reply
induced him to think that I was not much in favor of
that.   Said he again, " Charles, try it—there will be
no harm in that."   Knowing him to be kind, and
confident that he wished me well, I at last started.
I had not gone more than halfway when I turned back
a few steps; but I finally made up my mind to "try
my luck" as Mr. Campbell had suggested.   So I resumed my journey and soon entered Fort Union,
where I met Mr. McKenzie in the yard, not quite so
royally attired.   He came to meet me, and offered me
his hand.   After the usual compliments had been exchanged I remarked that I had not been apprised of
his intentions when he spoke of engaging me, and
that, thinking he wished to hire me as a common
hand, I had declined, having had enough of it; but
that, having been since informed to the contrary, I had
thought I would come to see him, and hoped there
was no harm done, in case no bargain were made.
To which he replied, " All right!   All right!   No, I
did not wish to engage you as a common hand.   I
wanted you for a clerk.   You will eat at my table, and
fare the same as myself.   Your work will be no other
than that which is the duty of all clerks in this country.   Now," he continued, " I will tell you how we

engage clerks—that is, inexperienced ones. We engage them for three years, for which term we give them $500 and a complete suit of fine broadcloth; but as you have been already one year in the country I will engage you for two years." These terms did not suit me; my strong inclination to go home made me feel quite independent, and I preferred to miss the bargain. I replied I did not feel like engaging for so long a term; but that I would engage for one year, and then, if he were pleased with me, and I with him, we should have no difficulty in arranging for another year. Finally he consented to this and the bargain was struck for one year, for which he allowed me $250 and a complete suit of clothes.

Bargain made [July 3, 1834],[12] I was almost sorry for it. I started back to Fort William, not after my wardrobe, which I could very well sacrifice, but to thank Mr. Campbell, and to bid adieu to my comrades. Mr. Campbell was extremely pleased to hear the result; he gave me a check for the amount due me, and after a long shake of the hand, with all his good wishes as well as those of my old messmates and others, I left Fort William. My load to Fort Union was not very encumbering; my old saddle bags, made of a yard of brown muslin, sewed at both ends with a

[12] " I entered in agreement on the third of July for one year at 250 $ per Anum "—says the Orig. Journ., in excellent Latin.

slit in the middle, containing two red flannel shirts, pretty well worn, and one check shirt, and one old white 3-point blanket, were about all I had brought to Fort Union;[13] my tin pan and cup I left behind.   I should have been ashamed to be caught there in my

[13] Fort Union was begun in the fall of 1829, under the direction of Kenneth McKenzie, and finished in 1833.   It was much damaged by a fire which occurred during its construction, Feb. 4, 1832.   It was for many years the headquarters and emporium of the A. F. Co.   Larpenteur, who now enters it as a humble clerk, was afterward in charge, and has more to say about it than any other.   We shall trace its history, from its rise through its culmination to its final fall, in his pages.

What is probably the best description which has ever appeared in print was furnished by Mr. Edwin T. Denig to Audubon on July 30, 1843, and published by the granddaughter of the illustrious naturalist, Miss M. R. Audubon, in the superb work which appeared in Dec., 1897, entitled Audubon and his Journals.   Mr. Denig's article occupies vol. ii, pp. 180–188.   I shall have frequent occasion to cite this work in connection with Larpenteur ; here I will give one passage which occurs in Mr. Denig's account:

"In the upper story are at present located Mr. Audubon and his suite.   Here from the pencils of Mr. Audubon and Mr. [Isaac] Sprague emanate the splendid paintings and drawings of animals and plants, which are the admiration of all ; and the Indians regard them as marvellous, and almost to be worshipped."

Audubon spent two months and four days of the summer of 1843 at Fort Union and in its vicinity ; his whole narrative is of exceptional interest in the present connection (vol. ii, pp. 28–154).   He is the most famous person who was ever there.   We may also remember that a princely personage, Maximilian of Wied, made Fort Union his headquarters in 1833 ; and hence "emanated," as Mr. Denig would say, some of those magnificent colored plates

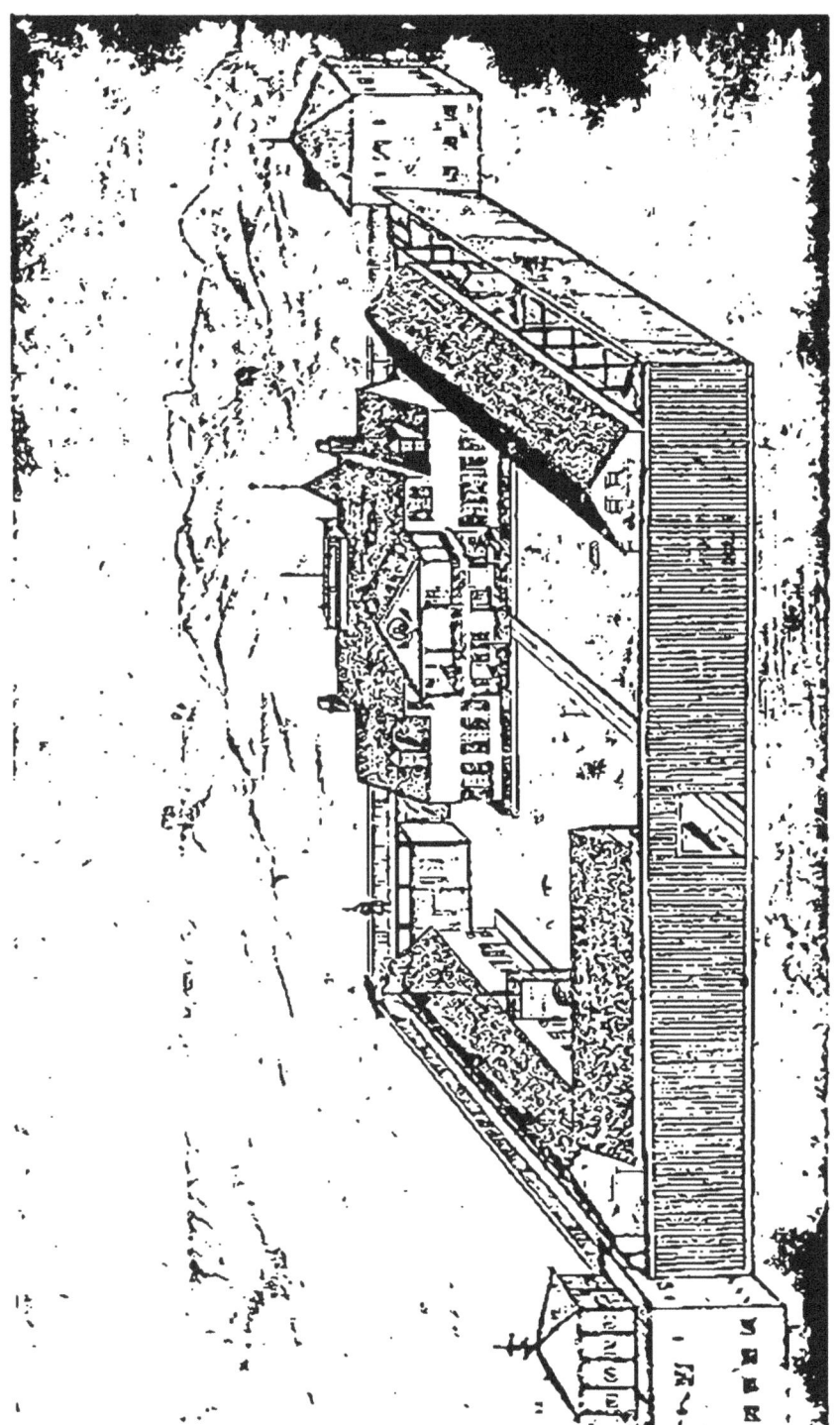

FORT UNION, 1864.

From a hitherto unpublished drawing.

skin suit, which was also sacrificed to Fort William.
Now I am at Fort Union, in the service of the great
American Fur Company.

which compose the folio atlas of the most luxurious souvenir of
Western adventure ever issued from the press.

George Catlin, who was here in 1832, rattles on about the place
in his peculiar fashion through Letters 2–9 of his work (4th ed.,
London, 1844, pp. 14–65); his pl. 3 gives an idea of the scenery,
but is worthless for the fort, which he furnishes with more than
two bastions.

A notice of Fort Union as it was in 1853, when visited by Isaac
I. Stevens on his exploration of routes near the 47th and 49th
parallels, begins on p. 85 of P. R. R. Reps., vol. xii, book i,
Washington, 1860, and is embellished with a colored lithograph,
pl. xvi.

Another good account, prepared by Mr. James Stuart at Fort
Peck in 1872–73, occupies Cont. Mont. Hist. Soc. i, 1876, pp.
80–84.

The picture of Fort Union which I am enabled to print
through the kindness of Dr. Matthews represents the post as it
was in 1864, and is probably the most accurate one which has
ever appeared. It was drawn by a soldier, name unknown.

CHAPTER V.

(1834-35.)

FORT UNION.

I MUST remark here that my dress was a little improved. I happened to have a pair of gray cassinette pants which I had brought from the States, and had seldom worn; that and my clean blue check shirt and my old cap were the only dress I possessed on entering Fort Union. All the clerks were strangers to me, and when the bell rang for supper I saw them put on their coats, for, as I found out afterward, they were not allowed to go to table in shirtsleeves. One of them, perceiving that I was coatless, was so kind as to lend me a coat, and so we started for supper. On entering the eating hall, I found a splendidly set table with a very white tablecloth, and two waiters, one a negro. Mr. McKenzie was sitting at the head of the table, extremely well dressed. The victuals consisted of fine fat buffalo meat, with plenty of good fresh butter, cream, and milk for those that chose; but I saw that only two biscuits were allowed to each one, as these were placed at each plate. I soon discovered, by the manner in which the clerks took their seats, that mine would come very near the end of the table, for it appeared to go by grade; but it was not many years until I reached next to head. I was hungry, and had such victuals been placed before me the day previous, while I was on horse guard, I should have played my part like a man. But among strangers I could not help being a little backward, and did not eat half to my satisfaction. As good luck would have it, some of the clerks used to take lunch before going to bed; so a large kettle of fat buffalo meat was put on to boil, and out of this I finished filling up. Then I went to bed with the expectation of curious dreams. What I dreamed I don't remember, neither do I now care. I awoke early, perhaps thinking in my sleep that I had my horses to turn out; but no, there were no horses for me to turn out. Mr. McKenzie, who played the nabob, went to bed late, and rose later, and as nothing could be served till he was ready, it was nine o'clock before we got to breakfast. But it came at last, and this morning I filled up fuller, with more ease.

Between ten and eleven, Mr. McKenzie sent his servant to tell me to call at the office. On entering he told me to sit down, and said, " Well, Larpenteur, we will assign you some little duty to try your hand upon, and if you prove faithful and attentive, as I hope and have all reason to believe you will, your salary will be increased next year, provided you wish to remain." My reply was that I hoped he would have no cause to complain. He then went to a place where the keys were hung, and handed me a bunch, saying, "Here are the keys of the fort gates, of the tool house and harness house, and of the bastions. Now it will be your duty to open the gates early in the morning, and lock them at night; to see that the tools and harness be kept in order, and all in their proper places; and you will also lend a hand, in case it should be required, about the stores." Such was my first employment at Fort Union.

Thus I went on quite easily for some time, and I thought my berth a very light one; but it was not long before I was promoted, and this made quite an addition to my former duties. Early in September, after all the hay had been hauled in, Fort William was to be rebuilt within 150 yards of Union. A clerk by the name of Moncrèvie,[1] who was at the time a trader, and also in charge of the men, had this to attend to; but he was a little too fond of whisky, and much too fond of the squaws, to do this work or any other as it should be done.

[1] Larpenteur commonly spells this name Moncravie, and I have found in print several other forms, as Moncrévie and Moncrévier, —in either case with or without acute or grave accent. The full name is believed to be Jean Baptiste Moncrèvie, and I shall adopt the latter form.

One afternoon, after the rebuilding of the fort had commenced, Mr. Hamilton, who was in charge at the time, went to see how it was progressing. The men had half of one side of the fort up, but it was an awful piece of work. The pickets were set in crooked, some too high, some too low, and the sight made the old gentleman furious. "Where is that Moncrèvie, that he is not here to attend to the work?" he asked. Being told that Moncrèvie had gone to the fort, he started off quite mad and rushed into our room, his nose appearing to have grown bigger on a sudden— for such was the case whenever he got out of humor. "Mr. Moncrèvie," he exclaimed, "why are you not with your men? That is a nice piece of work they are doing there!" Moncrèvie, all confused, was hurrying out, when the old gentleman said, "No! no! you need not go," and then turned round to me, saying, "Mr. Larpenteur, go and oversee that work and see if you cannot do better than that Mr. Moncrèvie." So I started, and when I got to the men they began to laugh, saying they expected as much. I told them that I was ordered to boss the job, of which they appeared to be glad. Then I ordered them to take all the pickets down, which was soon done, after which I had the trench straightened and the bottom leveled. Next day about noon Mr. Hamilton came to examine the work, and said, with the pleasant countenance he

could assume when he chose, " Oh! this looks something like work—not like what that good-for-nothing
Moncrèvie has been doing." At that time I had only
charge of the men allotted for the rebuilding of the
fort; but that same evening Mr. Hamilton sent for me
and said, " Larpenteur, I now wish you to take charge
of all the men, for that Moncrèvie will not do." Thus
came my first promotion. Notwithstanding this addition to my former duties I still thought my situation
pleasant, although it was, at times, rather disagreeable to command the men, and not infrequently some
fight would come off; but the most disagreeable part
of it was to come. Early in the fall trade commenced,
principally in jerked buffalo meat and tallow, both
mostly traded for liquor. The liquor business, which
was always done at night, sometimes kept me up all
night turning out drunken Indians, often by dragging
them out by arms and legs. Although the still house
had been destroyed, the Company found means to
smuggle plenty of liquor.

Before proceeding with my narrative I will detain
the reader to explain how it happened that the distillery was given up. A certain gentleman from the
Eastern States, by the name of Capt. Wheitte,[2] who

---

[2] Meaning Nathaniel J. Wyeth, who at the time of the incident
Larpenteur proceeds to relate was on his return from his first
expedition (1832-33), and had reached Fort Union Aug. 24, 1833,

had been on a tour to the Columbia, and returned by
way of the Bighorn and the Yellowstone in 1833,
reaching Fort Union about 10 days before we did,
thought proper to have better means of going down
the Missouri, and called on Mr. McKenzie to make
the necessary preparations for this journey. Mr.
McKenzie, who was a perfect gentleman, not suspecting the captain, who I cannot say was a spy,
did all he could to make his stay pleasant, showed all
the arrangements of the fort, explained how trade
was carried on, what immense profit was derived, and
also showed him the distillery. Capt. Wheitte ap-
appeared to be delighted to see this fine establishment, and probably would not have done what he did,
had he not found, when everything was in readiness

as we have already seen (note ⁴, p. 38). The story of the distillery does not appear in Irving's Bonneville, as Wyeth must have
had reason enough to keep such a piece of treachery to himself; but in chap. xli of Bonneville, where Wyeth's arrival at
Fort Union with Milton Sublette is given at the date just said,
Irving continues: "Here they were hospitably entertained by
Mr. M'Kenzie, the superintendent, and remained with him three
days, enjoying the unusual luxuries of bread, butter, milk, and
cheese, for the fort was well supplied with domestic cattle, though
it had no garden." Bvt. Major General Orlando B. Willcox,
U. S. A., informs me that Wyeth was a brother of his stepsons'
grandfather, of Cambridge, Mass.; one stepson, Nathaniel
Wyeth, being now a student at L'École des Beaux Arts in
Paris, and the other a student in the medical department of
Columbian University in Washington, D. C.

for his departure and he came to settle his bill, that
the charges were exorbitant. He said nothing,
settled, and started; but made it his business, as
soon as he arrived, to report Mr. McKenzie. A dispatch was sent up that winter for the distillery to be
destroyed. This was the last distillery in the Indian
country.

All went on as smoothly as could be expected
through our many drinking scrapes with Indians and
obstreperous Canadians. The time to re-engage came,
and pretty soon my case was carried to the office.
Mr. McKenzie said, " Well, Larpenteur, what do you
think? Will you hire for another year? " My reply
was, " I believe so, sir." " Well," said he, " if you
wish to remain, I will allow you $350 for this year."
" All right," was my answer. And now for another
year in the American Fur Company.

My first year [3] was not yet up, but all engagements
had to be made before the arrival of the steamer, and
the shipping of the returns; so that, in case any men
declined to re-engage, they could be sent off by one or
another conveyance. All the clerks were re-engaged
except Moncrèvie, who happened to be discharged.
Nothing took place worth mentioning until the fall, [4]

[3] His first year in the A. F. Co. would be up July 3, 1835; and
he is now re-engaged for 1835–36.

[4] Oct. 19, 1834, "when the Trappers returned from hunting

after the return of some of the free trappers. There was a half-breed family named Deschamps,[5] consisting of ten persons, among whom were the old man and three grown sons, who were in the habit of trapping, and were the very worst of subjects; and another half-breed family, headed by Jack Rem.[6] He had two sons-in-law, and a son 19 years of age, all of whom started on their trapping expeditions together, and returned together. It was customary, on their return from a hunt, to have a spree; and as they had been lucky the hunt was big, and so was the spree. They soon began a fight in which Jack Rem's son had his brains knocked out with the butt of a gun by one of the numerous and wicked Deschamps family. Mr. Lafferrier,[7] who was at the time the trader and storekeeper, became alarmed, for they began to threaten his life, and attempted to get liquor of him without paying for it. Mr. Hamilton, who was still in charge, did not know what to do to stop them, but at last advised Mr. Lafferrier to put laudanum in the whiskey. This advice was followed; they soon fell down and lay

after having sold there Beaver they got in to a Drinking spree and murdered a young man aged of 18 years," says Orig. Journ.

[5] Much more of this "numerous and wicked" family beyond, when we come to their violent deaths.

[6] This does not look right, but I can make nothing else of copy—possibly it should stand Jacques René.

[7] Spelling wavers in copy—perhaps intended for Leferrailleur.

stretched out on the ground in every direction, so
sound asleep that Mr. Hamilton became alarmed,
thinking the dose had been so strong that they would
never wake up again.   I happened not to be there at
the time, having that afternoon gone down to the garden, which was about three-quarters of a mile distant
from the fort.   Mr. Hamilton came there as fast as he
could, half scared to death, to tell me the story.   I
could not help laughing at the idea, and we immediately returned to the fort.   On my arrival I saw this
amiable family scattered along the river bank, still fast
asleep; but at dark they awakened and went home to
Fort William, where all those families were kept, as
were also some of the Company's men who had
squaws, and the horse guard with the horses.   Thus
this spree ended.   Nothing remarkable took place
until May of the following spring [1835].[8]   It was

---

[8] But the Orig. Journ. has a number of incidents prior to May,
1835.   I transcribe them in substance:

Nov. 15, 1834.   A party of Assiniboines under La Lance went
to war with the Grosventres of the Missouri; on the 23d they
were surrounded, 30 of them killed, and 10 wounded; fate of La
Lance uncertain, but he is supposed to have been killed.   It was
a sad sight—that of the wounded, who reached Fort Union after
a long journey, with hardly anything to eat and the thermome-
ter below zero.   The Assiniboines were greatly excited over this
defeat, and soon dispatched several war parties to surround and
if possible destroy the Grosventre village.

Nov. 30, 1834.   Eclipse of the sun noted at 11 a. m.   This I

customary, when buffalo got too far from the fort, for hunters to camp out, and from time to time send in loads of fresh meat. On such occasions all their families also went into camp to make dried meat for their own use, and also for a kind of recreation. Such a camp was called by the half-breeds of the north, who

have verified, and the important statement serves to fix Larpenteur's chronology thus far. He says that the fight began at that hour and lasted all day. On Dec. 22 he is informed by a trader that the Assiniboines only killed 4 and wounded 7 Grosventres. The latter, after the fight, stripped the Assiniboines. La Lance was dissected and his flesh given to the children to eat; his bones were bruised and boiled in a pot, and a bladder was filled with the marrow extracted from them. It appears that he had first been taken prisoner, and that before he was put to death he was subjected to "the most cruel act that Indians can ever invent."

Mar. 28, 1835. Fort Assiniboine, an outpost of Fort Union, was abandoned, and on Apr. 2 Mr. D. Lamont and the traders from that post arrived at Union by the steamer which had been obliged to winter at Assiniboine on account of low water. The returns they brought for the winter of 1834–35 were: 179 red foxes; 1,646 prairie do.; 18 cross do.; 74 badgers; 269 muskrats; 89 white wolves; 196 white hares; 5 swanskins; 4,200 buffalo robes; 37 dressed cowskins; 12 dressed calfskins; 450 salted tongues; 3,500 lbs. powdered and 3,000 lbs. dried buffalo meat.

Apr. 24, 1835. Mr. James Kipp arrived at Union from Fort McKenzie (the Blackfoot post near the mouth of Maria's river). His returns for the season were: 9,000 robes; 1,020 beavers; 40 otters; 2,800 muskrats; 180 wolves; 200 red foxes; 1,500 prairie-dogs; 19 bears; 390 buffalo tongues; all of which were brought down in a keel boat and two Mackinaws, with a force of 35 men.

May 1, 1835. Having thus written up his Journal, at this date Larpenteur goes on with regular day-by-day entries for 1835.

spoke broken French, mixed with many Cree words,
"nick-ah-wah"; and to go into it was "aller
en nick-ah-wah." It happened that, in this camp,
there was a beautiful half-breed by the name of
Baptiste Gardepie.[9] The Deschamps family, who
were there also, got jealous of him and, it was reported, had attempted to take his life. I will now
relate an affray which took place at the fort, while
they were in camp.

In the spring, after the trade was over, some strag-
glers always remained in camp at the fort, in spite of
all we could do to get them off; for they were great
nuisances, and it was dangerous for them to camp at
the fort on account of hostile Indians. Early in May
an express arrived from Fort Clark[10] by which we
were apprised that there would soon be a large war-
party of Gros Ventres and Mandans at Fort Union.
The chief wished to inform us of this and to warn our
young men not to sleep in any of the Indian lodges;
for, should there be any at the fort when the war-party
came, they would shoot into the lodges, but would not
like to kill any of the whites. So the young men were

[9] Jean Baptiste Gardepied (same word as now Gariépy): See
my Henry Journ., 1897, p. 872, for one of the name who went
with the overland Astorians in 1811.

[10] The important post of the A. F. Co. at the Mandans, for trading with those Indians, the Grosventres de Missouri, etc. More
about it in the sequel.

notified, and for my part I did all I could to induce
Mr. Hamilton to let the Indians sleep in the Indian
house, but he would not listen to me. There were
only two lodges of Indians, and almost every night,
unknown to the old gentleman, I let them into the
fort. But, fearing to be caught at this and thus dis-
please my boss, some nights I made them stay outside. It happened to be one of these nights that the
war party of Gros Ventres arrived about twelve
o'clock and fired into the two lodges. We heard the
shots plainly, and immediately the cry of "Open the
door!"—for there had been three white men in the
lodges at the time. On our entering them to ascer-
tain what damage had been done we found one squaw
dead, shot plumb through the heart; one shot through
both thighs; one through the calf of her leg, smashing
the shin bone; an old woman shot through the wrist;
a little boy 12 years of age shot through the bowels;
and one of the white men with two balls through the
left thigh, a little above the knee, cutting the artery.
He died the same morning at ten o'clock; the squaw
shot through the thighs died two days afterward, and
the little boy the next day—sad indeed was this affair!
Mr. Hamilton repented not letting them into the fort,
but it was too late—the damage had been done. But
the old Englishman was soon to see what could not be
called fun, and be badly put to his trumps.

About a week later a party of Assiniboines, who had
gone to war on the Gros Ventres and Mandans, arrived at Fort Union; and about ten o'clock at night a
rap was heard at the door.   As I was still doorkeeper,
I went to see who was there.   On asking who they
were, they replied that they were a war party of 20
men, on their return from the Gros Ventres.   At this
time all the wounded and well Indians were inside the
fort, and we were but few whites, as most of our men
were in camp.   Not thinking it prudent to let the Indians in, for fear of a row, I apprised Mr. Hamilton of
the arrival; but he told me to let them in if there were
but 20 men.   I suggested to him to send them to Fort
William, where there was no one at the time, the
families having all gone to camp; but, as usual, he
would not listen to me, and in I let them.   Soon afterward more knocking at the door was heard, and the
Indians in the fort said it was the balance of their
party, consisting of 70 men.   I went again to Mr.
Hamilton, who said, " Well, we may as well let the
balance in, for it may make matters worse to send
them to the other fort."   A little while after their entrance something unpleasant was evidently going to
happen, and from what I could understand it became
necessary to adopt means for our safety.   So I informed Mr. Hamilton of what was going on, upon
which the old gentleman, who had a sound old Eng-

lish head, told me to bring eight or ten muskets out
of the bastion and put them on the men's table in the
dining room; also to put one of the smallest cannon
in the passage of the main quarters.   This was to be
done with all care possible, that the Indians should
know nothing of it until the proper time came; for if
they saw us make such preparations, they might nip
his plan in the bud.   Very soon we were ready; the
window blinds of the dining room were opened, and
there could be seen by the three candles the bright
muskets, plenty of cartridges scattered over the table,
and four men ready for action.   The piece of artillery
was rolled back and forward in the passage, making a
tremendous noise, and two men mounted guard with
muskets and fixed bayonets.   Such preparations the
Indians had never seen or heard of before, and they
became, in their turn, more frightened than we had
been.   They had been very lively on the move and
very insulting at times, but they soon lay down and
went to sleep, or pretended to, so that all became
suddenly quiet.   Still, we did not feel quite safe; we
thought that perhaps they were shamming and that
they might try what they could do before morning.
This was about midnight.   To my great surprise, just
at the peep of day, I was called up; that was easily
done, for I was wide awake, with all my clothes on.
The partisan said that the Indians wished to go out,

and asked me to open the door for them; and in less than ten minutes not one of the party was left in the fort. One may imagine how relieved all hands were, when informed of this, for most of them had almost made up their minds that this would be their last night. As it was yet early, I told them to go and take a nap. I then went to Mr. Hamilton's room, and, after I had informed him of this, he said, "Well, Mr. Larpenteur, what do you think of my stratagem?" To which I replied that I felt confident it had been the means of saving our lives. "Yes, yes," said he; "now go to the cellar, fill this bottle with that good Madeira; we will have a glass, and then you will have time to take a little rest before breakfast, for I presume you have not slept much." I obeyed his orders, took a drink of Madeira, and went to bed. Thus ended the fright.

As I have had frequent occasion to mention Mr. "Hamilton,"[11] I will introduce him to the reader. His

[11] Dr. Matthews kindly contributes the following interesting note on Mr. Hamilton: "I never met this gentleman; but have heard much about him, and, when I have described him, you will understand why he was an object of wonder and gossip to the rude inhabitants of the Upper Missouri valley. He was an Englishman, of high social position at home, who for some reason saw fit to bury himself in the wilderness, though he never fell into the negligent habits of the country. Rumor made him a scion of nobility. He took no one into his confidence and was reticent as to his antecedents. He wore none

real name was Archibald Palmer. He was an English nobleman who, from some cause or other unknown to many, had been obliged to leave England and come to America, apparently without any means. How Mr. McKenzie became acquainted with him I am not able to say. Mr. Hamilton was a man of uncommon education, conversant with many subjects, and quite capable of keeping books. As Mr. McKenzie required a bookkeeper at Fort Union, he made arrangements with Mr. Hamilton to come here. What salary he received I never learned. Mr. Hamilton—as I shall continue to call him, for his real name was not known until after he left Fort Union and his English difficulties were over, when he resumed his proper name—was a man of fifty, who had habitually lived high, in consequence of which he had the gout. This brought him to the two extremes of being either

but the finest clothes, and always dressed in the latest London fashions. Every year, boxes were sent from London to St. Louis and thence forwarded to him at the mouth of the Yellowstone. Some of the French Canadians have told me, in tones of awe, that he took a bath and put on a clean shirt every day. He wore ruffled shirt-fronts, had a great gold chain around his neck, and was always polished, scented, and oiled to the highest degree. Long as he lived in the country, he never overcame his repugnance to Indians, whom he called 'beasts.' I have heard a tale of his angrily throwing a beautiful colored silk handkerchief (he carried no other kind) into the fire, because an admiring Indian had picked it up to examine it. He is mentioned in Catlin's N. A. Indians, vol. i, p. 21."

very pleasant or very crabbed, but, upon the whole, kept him crabbed; so he was not liked, though much respected. He remained a few years at Union, and died in St. Louis as cashier of the American Fur Company. I must say I got along remarkably well with him and was very sorry to learn of his death. Now I will return to my stories, of which I have many in store.

CHAPTER VI.

(1835-36.)

FORT UNION: CONTINUED.

A WEEK or ten days after the above-mentioned fright, the hunters were ordered to return; the camp was broken up, and all the half-breed families went into their former quarters in Fort William, as well as some of the company's men who had families, and were to take care of the horses. When they had all arrived and were reorganized, a conspiracy was gotten up, unknown to me, to kill old man Deschamps and his eldest son, François. The conspirators were Baptiste Gardepie, the two sons-in-law of Jack Rem, and Mr. Lafferrier—the latter a great hypocrite. This was in July, 1835. As Deschamps used to come to our room almost every morning after breakfast, the killing was to take place there. For this murderous work a rifle barrel was placed in the chimney corner, and Lafferrier put his dirk under his pillow, for Gardepie, who was to commence the job. François Deschamps, the son, was about 27 or 28 years old—

a fine stout young man; he was then interpreter for
Fort Union, and ate at the table with the boss and the
clerks. Soon after breakfast the father and son came
into our room, where the conspirators were already
assembled. It was a fine July morning [1] and I, knowing nothing of this, had taken a walk alone down by
the garden which was already progressing well, about
three-quarters of a mile from the fort. After some
little conversation, which naturally took place before
coming to the point, Gardepie got up and addressed
the old man, saying, " Deschamps, I want to know
now whether you will make peace or war with me;
you have frequently attempted my life, and I find it
necessary to ask you this question—now, what is your

[1] Thursday, July 23, 1835, is the date of this homicide given in the
Orig. Journ., which narrates the tragedy much more circumstan-
tially, but to the identical effect. The extermination of the rest
of the Deschamps family comes later on. François sen., with
his three sons, François jun., Charles, and Joseph, had returned
to Fort Union from their trapping on Wednesday, June 10, 1835.
The quarrel between François junior and Gardepied Larpenteur
understood to be about a squaw belonging to Gardepied. François fell in love with her, and his father advised him to offer
Gardepied a horse for her. This grieved Gardepied, who swore
that either he or a Deschamps should die for it. He dared any
one of them to fight ; they would not accept the challenge, but
one of them sought to kill Gardepied, and would have shot him
through a window had not an Indian interfered. Next day
Gardepied made up his mind to have a settlement with the Deschamps; and how he effected it Larpenteur proceeds to say.

answer?" To which old Deschamps replied, " I will never make peace with you as long as there is a drop of blood in my veins." Some blood was quickly out of his veins, for Gardepie immediately seized the rifle barrel and struck a fatal blow on the old man's head. Then he turned round to the son, and, with another blow, knocked him down. But this wound not being a mortal one, François made out to creep under one of the beds, where he begged for his life until the conspirators took pity on him. Gardepie was induced to desist from killing him; but, not thinking that the father had been mortally struck, he reached for the dirk and ripped the old man's bowels out—which operation was not necessary. All this was done in a very short time. Returning from the garden and approaching our quarters I observed that the curtains were down, which was an unusual thing, and when I came to open the door I found it locked on the inside. At my request it was immediately opened to admit me, but directly closed again. The door being shut and curtains down, I could not at first discover what had taken place, but soon saw a sheet spread on the floor and knew there was a corpse under it. On looking about, I saw young François Deschamps sitting at a table with his head held down in his hands, which were still all bloody. No one else was in the room but Gardepie, who said, " I have settled with the old man, and I would have done the same with this coward here, had he not begged so hard for his life." I made no reply, though, of course, I pitied the poor fellow, who was so near the corpse of his father, and uncertain as yet of his own life. It was a sad sight. Mr. Lafferrier, who, as I have already remarked, was a great hypocrite and had thus acquired his popularity among the Indians and half-breeds, had gone to the fort with the pipe of peace, to try to bring about a reconciliation between those two families; and in this he finally succeeded. The old man was buried the same day, and to all appearances everything went on as usual.

It was thought that this peace would last, as Jack Rem's family was considered revenged by the death of the old man, and had thus been made nearly equal in strength to that of the Deschamps. What afterward induced us to think the peace would be kept was that Gardepie went on a beaver hunt with the three young Deschamps and never offered to molest them. Michel Gravel and Little Frenchman were the names of Jack Rem's two sons-in-law who went the following fall [1835] on their hunt on Milk river, which abounded with beaver, and, like all beaver trappers, fell in with a war party of Blackfeet, by whom they were both killed. This accident reduced Jack's family considerably and enabled the Deschamps to show their wicked dispositions again. But before describing a big battle which took place the following summer [1836], I will relate a little story to show you how cunningly and quickly Indians can work destruction, and also give the character of Gauché, Robert Campbell's chief, whom I have already called Cohan (Hurry Up). Gauché was his French name, which means Left Hand. But by his tribe he was called Meenah-yau-henno,[2] meaning the One who Holds the Knife—with which they said he could cut a rock in two, owing to his strong medicine. As I have already remarked, Hurry Up was feared by all the surrounding tribes, and was called by the whites the Wild Bonaparte. The old fellow had been so successful in his warfare that he found no difficulty in raising the number of warriors he wanted. At this time he had raised a party of 250 to 300, to make war on the Blackfeet, who were very rich in horses. Being considered so great a medicine man and warrior, he had no trouble with his young men, and could order the rush as he thought proper. On this their success always depends, for Indians seldom stand a long battle, and when they do it does not amount to much. About the middle of March the old man came within

---

[2] See note [3], p. 55, where it is said that De Smet gives this name as Mina-yougha. In Riggs' Dictionary *mína* = knife, and *yuhá* = to have, own, possess.—W. M.

one day's march of Fort McKenzie, where he fell on
the trail of a camp of Blackfeet, containing about
30 lodges, on the way to their fort to make their last
spring trade. The old fellow could tell by the looks
of things in their camping-place that they were rich
in trade-goods and in horses, and that a big drunk
would be sure to take place ; for the Blackfeet are
great drunkards. After the chief had well examined everything about the camping grounds he went
to work at his medicine. He then told his people
that he had seen a great deal of blood on the enemy's
side, but very little on theirs, and that most, if not all
of them, would return on horseback with many scalps,
if they would obey his commands. The old fellow
was not mistaken. They soon approached the Blackfoot camp, which was near the fort, making ready for
a big spree. It was Gauché's intention to rush on the
camp when they should be at the height of the spree,
too drunk to defend themselves. When it was near
daylight the order was given for the rush, and so well
was it executed that in a very short time few were left
alive in camp, and all the horses were captured with
ease—as we learned, upward of 300 head. So great
and glorious was the old man's campaign ; and then
it was " Co-han! hurry up! let us go home and dance
the scalp dance "—for many were the scalps they had
taken of men, women, and children. We will let

them go and I will return to the little story I promised to relate.

There was an old Assiniboine who had remained after our last trade, with the intention, as he said, to go down to Fort Clark in the steamer, although no peace as yet had been made between the Assiniboines and the Gros Ventres. In the meantime a war party of about 150 Blackfeet, all on horseback, came to Fort Union in search of the Assiniboines, to be revenged on the camp of old Co-han ; this was about the 1st of June,[3] and at that season men were always scarce in the fort, as most of them were required to take down the returns. So we would not allow more than 20 Indians at a time in the fort. The partisan and other important men in the Blackfoot party commenced by making a great deal of the old man, smoking with him, and telling him that they were in search of the Assiniboines with the intention of making peace with them, and that they would be very glad if he would go with them. They also said they had some fine horses which were intended for the Assiniboines, in case they would make peace, and if he would go with them they would make him a present of a nice pony. They did all they could to persuade him to go, and we did all we could to put him out of

[3] June 12, 1836, by Orig. Journ., where a long story is made of the treacherous murder of the poor old Assiniboine.

the notion. Finally the time came for them to start, and not finding the old fellow quite decided, they sent in a beautiful pony, saddled and bridled, telling him it should be his if he would come along. The old man was tempted, mounted the pony, and started. By this time most of the party had left, and were seated on the hills back of the fort, awaiting the rest, and expecting that the old Assiniboine would be along with them; there were also 12 or 15 young men mounted on ponies, ready apparently to serve as an escort for the old man. As soon as I had turned him out—for I was still the doorkeeper—I made haste to run up on the bastion to see what would happen. The escort had not gone over 200 yards from the fort before they fired a volley into the old man, who fell dead off his pony, and in less than no time was scalped. After they had all reached the hills they made us signs that there was no danger for us, and disappeared. I then took a party of six or seven men, wrapped the old man in his robe, and stuck him up in a large elm tree to dry, as this was their own custom.

Now, reader, make ready for the battle, as it will soon come off. In the latter part of June,[4] shortly

---

[4] June 28, 1836, is the date given in the Orig. Journ., in a long special article headed "Distruction of the Des Champ.s family," no doubt the most circumstantial and reliable we possess. As old Deschamps was the one who dispatched Governor Robert

after the last-mentioned affray took place, the company's steamboat arrived. After her departure, it was customary to have a big drunk throughout. At this time there were between 60 and 70 men at the fort. The half-breeds who were in Fort William with some of our own men also got gloriously drunk. About midnight old Mother Deschamps said to her children, " Now, my sons, if you are men, you will revenge the death of your father." This struck

Semple, in the massacre on the Red River of the North, June 19, 1816, the fate of this family of rakehellions becomes a matter of some historic moment, aside from the dramatic force of the final tragedy. We have already seen that old François Deschamps was killed by Gardepied, July 23, 1835, and Larpenteur now proceeds to the affair which finished the precious progeny from midnight of June 28, when it began with the killing of Jack Rem by the young Deschamps, to some late hour of June 29. Several versions, with conflicting dates, if any, have appeared : see for example Maximilian, English ed., 1843, p. 276, and my Henry, 1897, p. 557, where my note is incorrect in some particulars, and must be checked by the present account. We cannot here go into the voluminous legal testimony of the Semple affair; but it appears from the deposition of Louis Nolan, clerk H. B. Co., on p. xlii of Selkirk's Statement, 8vo, London, 1817, that Deschamps was the one who did kill the Governor, after the latter had been wounded by Cuthbert Grant. I will transcribe some passages from Larpenteur's Orig. Journ., neglecting his peculiarities of spelling, for comparison with or in amplification of the narrative given above:

" This wicked family was obliged to emigrate from the Red river on account of its bad conduct. I have been informed by several persons from Red river that in the time of the battle bethem favorably, and being in liquor they immediately killed old Jack Rem, swore they would also kill all the half-breeds whom they considered his friends, and even threatened the whites in the fort. This took place about midnight, when the spree in Fort Union had subsided and all hands had gone to sleep. I was awakened by loud raps and voices at the door, which latter I could distinguish to be those of females, crying, "Open the door! quick—they are fighting—they have killed my father." They were the widow of

tween the English and the half-breeds François Deschamps, the father of the family, had committed the most cruel acts that any human being can be guilty of. After the battle he was seen on the battle ground with his gun shooting those which were wounded. Some of those poor creatures would request of him a little time to pray, which he would allow, in saying, ' Make haste, you d—d son of a b—h,' and when he thought the prayer was long enough he would shoot them down and rob them of what they possessed. It has also been reported that it was him that killed the governor. They came on the Missouri about nine years ago [*ca.* 1827], from which time they conducted themselves the worst that any family could do. The family consisted of ten children and the nephew of their father, of which there were three grown sons [François jun., Charles, and Joseph], and two boys of from fourteen to fifteen years of age."

It appears among their crimes that they had twice robbed Fort Union; robbed Mr. Jeanisse and threatened to kill him; robbed and whipped Indians; murdered a young man in 1834; and habitually committed adultery with their sisters-in-law. Such deviltries were often instigated by both parents, who seem to have been more adept in crime than any of their offspring lived to become.

Michel Gravel and her mother, the wife of Jack Rem.[5]
I had not shut the door before eight or ten of our men
came running in great fury, swearing vengeance
against the Deschamps family, all of whom they
would destroy, big and small. They raised all hands,
and in a body went to Mr. McKenzie, of whom they
demanded arms and ammunition in angry tones, de-
claring they were determined to put an end to the
Deschamps family. This demand was made in such
terms that Mr. McKenzie could not well refuse, fearing the consequences, and not being himself much
averse to their intention. Having been furnished
with a cannon, muskets, and ammunition, they went

[5] This preliminary murder is somewhat differently given in the
Orig. Journ. Ignoring as before Larpenteur's peculiarities of
diction, it stands as follows : "Mr. D. D. Mitchell, who had two
or three years ago married [one of] their [Deschamps'] sisters,
returned on the steamboat, and taken his wife again, gave them
considerable presents, which induced them to believe that they
would be supported by him in case they might kick up a fuss.
Sure enough, next evening when the boat landed they traded
some porcupine-work to the hands of the boat for liquor, and
commenced drinking. About twelve o'clock at night I was
awakened by a discharge of guns from the old fort and immediately got out of bed. Some one knocked at the door, which I
opened; it was the daughter of Jack Kipling, who, crying bitterly,
informed me that the Deschamps had killed her father, and shot
at her and the men who were guarding the horses." Thus the
two accounts differ as to who was killed, unless " Rem " and
" Kipling " are different names of the same person.

to work. But, in the first place, all the horses and
all the company's effects were removed from the fort,
and before the fight commenced the Deschamps were
required to turn out their squaws, who were Assiniboine women, whom we did not want to kill for fear
of the tribe. Thinking the fight would not take place
as long as they kept in the squaws, they refused to
turn them out. After allowing them what time we
thought necessary to make up their minds on this
subject, the order to fire was given. As we had a
cannon we supposed they would not go into the bastions, and as we found their shots were only fired out
of their own dwellings we aimed altogether at these
houses. When they found we were determined to
put our threats into execution they turned out their
squaws, who told us that we had already killed one
man, but that it would be difficult for us to destroy
them all, as they had dug holes under the floors,
where our balls could not reach them. Yet we kept
constantly firing into the houses, until at last the old
lady herself came out with the pipe of peace, begging
for her life and that of her children; but she was shot
through the heart in stepping out of the fort.[6] As

---

[6] By a half-breed named J. Mayotte. At that moment one of
her sons was already dead in the house. The nephew was next
shot by a young half-breed named Jean Marchaud, in the house
of Gardepied and Jack Kipling, where he had taken refuge.

she was holding her pipe straight in front of her when she was hit, she fell precisely on top of it, at which the boys exclaimed in great mirth, "There's an end to the mother of the devils." In the meantime our firing was kept up; but few shots were heard from them, and at last some of our party ventured into the fort, thinking they were all killed; but that was a mistake. They commenced firing again, and our side made a double-quick retreat; but one [7] of them was shot through the neck as he was stooping through the small door of the fort. It was by this time getting rather late in the day, and it was feared that the fight might continue until night, under cover of which they could make their escape, which would prove serious to the Company in future; and as the bloody work had been begun, it was obliged to be accomplished. In order to do so it was thought proper to set the fort on fire, with the view of burning them in it; but for fear that some might escape through the fire, the hunter of the fort and several other good horsemen were mounted on the best horses to run them down like buffalo, should they make such an attempt. These precautions having been taken, a

[7] This was one Mayotte. Another half-breed, Joseph Vivié or Vivier, was shot in the wrist, and later killed by a shot through the heart from François, who had meanwhile taken refuge in one of the bastions.

fire was started; as the fort was dry it soon began to blaze, and in a little while the houses were consumed. We saw one man run out of them and take refuge in the east bastion, into which the cannon was fired several times, but the ball went through without other damage than making its hole. Meanwhile the fire stopped, having burned only one side of the fort and the houses; so the bastion stood with this individual inside it, and was dangerous to approach. One of our men [Vivić], wanting to display his bravery, went near it to get a good shot through the cracks; but this cost him his life. A shot through the heart made him jump up about six feet in the air and fall dead on the spot, on which a loud yell was heard from the man in the bastion. The firing on our side was renewed faster than ever, until it was found that no shot was fired out of the bastion, when some of the boldest of our party determined to see if the individual inside it was dead or alive. On entering the bastion they discovered him backed up in one corner; they immediately fired and he fell dead. This was François Deschamps, the last survivor, as all the rest had been burned or shot in the houses. After he was brought out we found that he had a broken wrist and was out of ammunition. Had he not been thus disabled and defenseless he would probably have killed several of us and made his escape. The men thought he might go, like the balance, into flames; so they threw him into the fire with one of his brothers, and both were burned to ashes. A hole was dug, into which the old woman was put without any ceremony. Thus the battle ended, about sunset, in the death of eight of the family.[8] The youngest son, about ten years of age, after being wounded, was suffered to come out; but he died the next day. Such was the end of this troublesome family, after which peace and comfort were enjoyed.

Now, as I have remarked, all was quieted. Outfits were made up and started for the Blackfeet and Crows, and we were left with none but the men allotted for Fort Union, numbering about 30, all told. These were assigned to their several duties, including the horse guard, for which a Mexican, a Dutchman, and a Canadian named Tibeau were appointed. The Mexican was not fit for anything else; the Dutchman was very green in one sense, and very white in another, as will be seen presently. All went on peaceably until about the middle of September [1836], when the Mexican thought he would take a ride back to Mexico on the best horse in the band, and picked

---

[8] "Not a crueler death than they deserved," says the Orig. Journ., "but much crueler than I wished to witness. Their sister, the wife of Mr. Mitchell, and a younger sister of hers went to the Blackfeet with her husband, also a little brother of about five years of age; the elder boy was taken to St. Louis."

out the green Dutchman to assist him in the execution of his plans.   But it seems that they both were tolerably green.   On one fine day they proposed to Tibeau to go to their dinner first, saying that they would not be long, and that he could go afterward and stay in the fort as long as he pleased.   The proposition was accepted by Tibeau, and off started the two gentlemen, who, sure enough, were not gone long; and immediately on their return Tibeau went to his dinner. At this early time the guard was kept up more with a view to prevent the horses from straying away than for fear of their being stolen by hostile Indians. This induced Tibeau to delay; but, fearing that he might be hurried out of the fort by the proper authorities, which he had reason to believe would be done rather roughly, he at last started back.   On his return to the guard he could see neither of the two men; but, thinking that they might have gone a little way, made nothing of it and began to look around. Still seeing nothing of them, he commenced to hallo; but no answer was heard.   Then he began to surmise that things were not all right, the men having been so willing to remain, and thought he would examine the band of horses.   He soon discovered that the two best American horses were missing.   Yet, as all the men were in the habit of strolling in search of antelope, and sometimes for pleasure, he waited a while, thinking they would soon make their appearance; but no one came, and he finally went to report the matter. Men were immediately sent in search of the thieves. Thinking that the Mexican would attempt to cross the river above, the men were first ordered up, but returned at night, having seen no tracks. Instead of going up, as it was thought they had, the Mexican and his man had concealed themselves in the point below the fort, it being his plan to steal the ferryboat at night and cross over. That night they came within three-quarters of a mile below the fort, where the Mexican left the Dutchman with the horses, while he went after the ferryboat. But when he came to the fort, it seems that he got scared at the barking of the dogs and could find no opportunity to get the boat off. When day was about breaking, he concluded to abandon that project and returned to the Dutchman, whom he found sound asleep and the horses gone. By this time it was daylight, and fearing to be discovered if they should attempt to look for the horses, they thought it advisable for each one to do as he thought proper. The Dutchman decided to give himself up to the mercy of the authorities; the Mexican concluded to try his luck at large for a while. When the door of the fort was opened one of the men, who happened to go out first, saw two horses near the hills, and came to me saying, " There are two horses which look very much like the stolen ones." I immediately sent after them, and to be sure they were the very two—Mr. McKenzie's favorite horse and the next best, a fine iron-gray. The question then was, What had become of the men? Some thought one thing, and some another, but none guessed right. Soon after breakfast Mr. Dutchman appeared, all in a tremble, and commenced to make up a story which had neither head nor tail. Not even giving him time to finish it, Mr. McKenzie requested me to take his gun from him, and put him in irons in the blacksmith shop. This was done immediately. He knew not what had become of the Mexican. Four or five days after this the Mexican came to deliver himself up, saying, " Mr. McKenzie, I have done wrong; here I am, do with me what you choose; but please don't send me to the States." Without replying to him Mr. McKenzie requested me to have him ironed and placed in confinement with the Dutchman, to await trial. Four days afterward they were tried, convicted, and sentenced to receive thirty-nine lashes. So they were tied to the flagstaff to take their punishment. The Dutchman was flogged first. When stripped to the waist his skin looked fair and tender, and was actually so; for at every blow the blood flew at such a rate that his sentence was reduced one-half. But the Mexican's hide was brown and tough; he hardly groaned, and received the full number of lashes. Both were soon taken to the States by James Beckwith,[9] the great mulatto brave among the Crows, whose life was published some time afterward. Thus ended this scrape.

[9] James P. Beckworth or Beckwourth. Life and Adventures of, written from his own dictation by T. D. Bonner ; orig. ed., N. Y., 1856, 12mo, pp. 357; new ed., with preface and notes by Charles G. Leland ("Hans Breitmann"), London and N. Y., 1892, 8vo, pp. 440, plates. It is a good story, founded on fact, but may be best enjoyed by one who does not care to sift fiction ; still, it contains a great deal of information which may be relied on to some extent, though most of it requires to be corroborated or confirmed from other sources. Beckwourth appears to have been repeatedly at Fort Union, and on p. 313, 2d ed., speaks of leaving that post for St. Louis; but I cannot connect this incident with Larpenteur's statement, owing to lack of dates.

CHAPTER VII.

(1836-38.)

FORT UNION: CONTINUED.

HAVING frequently mentioned Mr. McKenzie [1] as a member of the American Fur Company, I will give him a more ample introduction to the reader. Kenneth McKenzie was born in Scotland of very respectable parents, and was some near connection of the great explorer, Sir Alexander McKenzie. He en-

[1] The only Kenneth McKenzie who became generally known in the N. W. Co. was the one who was drowned in Lake Superior in 1816: see my Henry Journal, 1897, p. 930. At that time the Kenneth McKenzie of whom Larpenteur speaks, and who became so prominent in the A. F. Co. on the Missouri, was a very young man who had not made any mark—probably a clerk N. W. Co., who first appears a few years after the date said. Larpenteur has him with substantial accuracy, I think. He did trade on the Upper Mississippi, having left the N. W. Co., after 1821, and was bought out by the A. F. Co. about 1827. His precise relationship to the other Kenneth McKenzie, and to Sir Alexander McKenzie, I have not ascertained; but he was some sort of a cousin of the latter. He was born in Scotland in 1801, and died at St. Louis in 1861. His son, Owen McKenzie, appears beyond, in life and death. His unmarried daughter now (1898) resides

gaged to the Northwest at the time that Company was formed to oppose the Hudson Bay Company. It was the custom to engage clerks for the term of three years; but after they had served seven, they had the privilege of entering the Company as partners. Those young men had to be of good standing and bear good characters. The Northwest could not compete with the strong Hudson Bay Company and were finally [in 1821] obliged to abandon the country.[2] Mr. McKenzie, who had taken some liking to the trade and thought there was money in it, struck off for the upper waters of the Mississippi, in the regions where

in St. Louis, where a valuable collection of his papers and other effects was destroyed by fire.

James Stuart says, Cont. Mont. Hist. Soc., i, 1876, p. 88: " In 1822 he went to New York, and got an outfit of Indian trade goods on credit, and established a trading post on the Upper Mississippi, and remained in that part of the country till 1829 [?], when he came to the Missouri and established Ft. Union. He was in charge of all the Northwestern fur trade until 1839, when he resigned—Alexander Culbertson taking his place—and went to St. Louis, where he went into the wholesale liquor trade, and lived there until he died in 1856 or 1857 [not till 1861]. He was a man of great courage, energy, good judgment, and great executive ability. His wife now [1875] resides in St. Louis."

[2] Hardly that—but they were obliged to abandon their organization and be merged in the invincible H. B. Co. Most of the persons concerned remained in the country in business under the new régime. What happened to the N. W. Co. in 1821 was precisely the issue they forced upon the X. Y. Co., Nov. 5, 1804: particulars in Henry Journ., 1897, p. 255.

the American Fur Company was carrying on trade, in small furs particularly, to a great extent. Whether he had any means at the time I am unable to say, and also in what capacity he entered the American Fur Company; but he probably came in as a member, and they soon placed unbounded confidence in him. Having served the Northwest, he had become acquainted with the manner in which trade was carried on in the north, and also with the tribes in that region. He soon persuaded the American Fur Company to extend their trade on the Upper Missouri, for he knew that the Hudson Bay Company did not and could not trade buffalo robes, which would not pay for transportation over their portages, and that their trade was entirely confined to fine furs. This idea in regard to extending trade was correct, but the distance was tremendous, as those going up had to be towed in keel boats a distance of 2,000 miles. But, as I have remarked, the persuasion of Mr. McKenzie, and the unbounded confidence they had in him, overcame all difficulties. About the year 1827 an outfit was made up and started for the mouth of the Yellowstone, Mr. McKenzie in charge. They did not reach that far the first year, but established a wintering post [1827-28] at the mouth of White river, halfway between Forts Union and Berthold—say 150 miles below the Yellowstone. After the post was finished

Mr. McKenzie started for the States, and Mr. Honoré Picotte remained in charge. The returns were found encouraging, and the following year [1829] he went on to the mouth of the Yellowstone, where the chief of the band of the Rocks[3] had desired him to build, and which was a beautiful site, abounding in the best of timber, above, below, and opposite the fort, and with all kinds of game. Mr. McKenzie made this his residence and very soon messengers were dispatched north, inviting all Assiniboines, Crees, and Chippewas to the Missouri. When they learned that Mr. McKenzie was there it was not long before large numbers of these Indians came over, together with many half-breed families. Next year [1830] he determined to extend the trade, both up the Missouri for the Blackfeet and up the Yellowstone for the Crows. As to the Crows there was no difficulty, but the Blackfeet, who were deadly enemies to the Americans, he could not well manage against their will, nor did he think it advisable to start up an outfit before learning how they were disposed. It happened at the time[4] that there was

[3] One of the divisions of Assiniboines: see my Henry Journ., 1897, p. 523.

[4] "At the time" is the winter of 1330-31, as we learn from Cont. Mont. Hist. Soc. i, 1876, p. 84, where we read further: "McKenzie . . sent a party of four men—Burger [*sic*], Dacoteau, Morceau, and one other man—in search of the Indians, and to see

then at the fort an old trapper named Berger, who had
been in his young days in the employ of the Hudson

if there was sufficient inducements to establish a trading-post.
The party started up the Missouri river with dog-sleds, to haul
a few presents for the Indians. . . They followed the Missouri
to the mouth of the Marias river, thence up the Marias to the
mouth of Badger creek, without seeing an Indian, finding plenty
of game of all kinds, and plenty of beaver in all the streams running into the Missouri.   Every night when they camped they
hoisted the American flag, so that if they were seen by any Indians
during the night they would know it was a white man's camp ;
and it was very fortunate for them that they had a flag to use in
that manner, for the night they camped at the mouth of Badger
creek they were discovered by a war-party of Blackfeet, who
surrounded them during the night, and as they were about firing
on the camp, they saw the flag and did not fire, but took the
party prisoners.   A part of the Indians wanted to kill the whites
and take what they had, but through the exertions and influence
of a chief named ' Good-woman,' they were not molested in
person or property, but went in safety to the Blackfoot camp on
Belly river, and stayed with the camp until spring.   During the
winter they explained their business, and prevailed upon about
one hundred Blackfeet to go with them to Union to see McKenzie.
They arrived at Union about the 1st of April, 1831, and McKenzie
got their consent to build a trading-post at the mouth of the
Marias.   The Indians stayed about one month, then started
home to tell the news to their people.   McKenzie then started
[James] Kipp, with 75 men and an outfit of Indian goods, to
build a fort at the mouth of the Marias river, and he had the fort
completed before the winter of 1831[-32].   It was only a temporary arrangement to winter in, in order to find out whether it
would pay to establish a permanent post.   Next spring [1832]
Col. [David D.] Mitchell (afterward colonel in Doniphan's expedition to Mexico) built some cabins on Brule bottom, to live in

Bay Company, at the Fort of the Prairie,[5] when Mr.
John Rowand was in charge; and this having been
a post for the Blackfeet, he had acquired the language

till a good fort could be built. The houses at the mouth of the
Marias were burned after the company moved to Brule bottom.
Alex. Culbertson was sent by McKenzie to relieve Mitchell and
to build a picket-stockade fort 200 feet square on the north bank
of the Missouri, which he completed during the summer and fall
of 1832. This fort was occupied for eleven years, until Ft. Lewis
[or Louis] was built by Culbertson on the south side of the Missouri river, near Pablois' island, in the summer of 1844. Fort
Brule [Brulé: otherwise called Fort Piegan and Fort McKenzie, or
known as the Blackfoot post] was then abandoned and burned.
In 1846 Ft. Lewis was abandoned, and Ft. Benton was built by
Culbertson, about seven miles below Ft. Lewis, and on the north
bank of the river."

I have cited this account in fixing the date of the interesting
story Larpenteur proceeds to relate, which is thus seen to be
corroborated in all essential particulars—the principal variations
in fact being that Mr. James Stuart sends only four men on the
diplomatic mission, though Larpenteur implies that they were
a dozen; and more than doubles the number of Blackfeet whom
Larpenteur brings in. McKenzie's genius was perhaps never
better displayed than in this great stroke of business, which had
far-reaching commercial, political, military, and even ecclesias-
tical consequences, in the development of the whole region over
which his operations extended.

[5] One of several Forts des Prairies on the N. Saskatchewan,
probably that at Edmonton. Much about this Mr. Rowand will be
found in my Henry Journal, p. 602 and following. I have lately
corresponded with his granddaughter, Miss Sophie H. Rowand,
who resides at No. 30 St. Patrick Street, Toronto, Ont. One or
more persons named Berger are noted, *ibid.*, p. 594.

and could speak it fluently.   So Mr. McKenzie proposed to send Berger to the Blackfeet, to try to bring
down a party with whom he would endeavor to make
a treaty before sending up an outfit.   Berger consented; but as this undertaking was extremely dangerous, Mr. McKenzie would not take it upon himself to order any of the men on the expedition.   Not
less than 12 men would do; but there was no difficulty
in raising the required number of volunteers, who
were soon ready for the march.   The forlorn hope,
as they were called, started with the American flag
unfurled, hardly expecting to return.   But Mr. Mc-
Kenzie was in good hopes, for they were young Canadians, who knew not a word of English, and the
Blackfeet were accustomed to them, as they were also
employed by the Hudson Bay Company.   He anticipated no danger, except that of being surprised by a
war party while encamped, which was also Berger's
fear.   Having searched for the Blackfeet for about
four weeks, the men were at last so fortunate as to discover a large camp, without being discovered themselves; and the time had come to try their pluck.
" Blackfeet in sight—that awful tribe, of whom we
have heard so many terrible stories—what is going to
be our fate? " was the talk.   Some moves were made
to abandon the idea of entering the camp, and to ske-
daddle if possible; but old man Berger was grit, and

succeeded in getting his men along. He knew the Indian customs as well as their language; the men put great confidence in him, and determined to follow, saying, " Now for the butcher shop!" Berger took the lead with the flag bearer by his side, and his little frightened party close in the rear. Soon after they had got on their march they were discovered, and in less time after that a large party of mounted Indians were making for them at full speed. Berger, having caused his little party to stop, advanced with the flag bearer. The Indians, perceiving this maneuver, and not knowing what to make of it, paused for a while. Berger advanced, and when at a hearing distance cried out his name; at which they rushed up to shake hands, and the party which had kept their position were ordered to come up. How their pulses quickened and their hearts thumped is not hard to imagine, for fear had not entirely left them, and they did not know what fate was reserved for them in the Blackfoot camp. They would have preferred to turn back, but it was too cowardly as well as too late, and on they had to go. On entering camp there was great yelling and shouting in all directions; but after this had subsided they were lodged, feasts commenced, and all was done in such a friendly manner that the boys began to feel reassured. When Berger had made his intentions known, a party of 40 Indians consented to accompany him to the Yellowstone. None of them had ever been there, and some showed a little reluctance; at which Berger, in order to induce them to come, represented the distance to be somewhat shorter than it really was. The party was soon ready, and they all set off. Then came trouble and renewed fear in camp, for the Indians soon commenced to complain of the distance, thinking a trap had been laid by the whites to destroy them, and it was with great difficulty that Berger could make them agree to proceed. Things began to look rather dark, but at last they consented to go on a few days more. One night, when they had come within one day's march of the fort, as Berger knew very well, the Indians swore they would go no further—that he had lied to them, and they would have revenge. Berger was put to his trumps; but, being sure of reaching the fort next day, made them a speech, saying, " I tell you you will be in the fort to-morrow, smoking the pipe of peace with the great chief who sent me. Here I am with my party and horses; if I don't bring you to the fort to-morrow, you are welcome to my scalp and all the horses." This struck them with a great deal of force, and they consented to go on another day. Next morning an early start was made to give ample time to finish the journey, and about three in the afternoon they arrived on a ridge, in full view of the fort, where they sat down to smoke and vermilion themselves. Soon they saw the large flag hoisted, heard the cannon firing, and a little while after that the forlorn hope, with all the Blackfeet, entered Fort Union. In course of time a treaty was made, and next spring [1831] an outfit was started under Mr. James Kipp,[6] with instructions to build at the mouth of Maria's river, which was the first trading post established for the Blackfeet, and called Fort McKenzie.[7] Fort Cass was built next spring [1832]; and

[6] Long a well-known person in the fur trade of the Missouri and Yellowstone. In 1847 he was a hardy veteran, upward of 65 years old, who for many years had had a farm near Independence, Mo., and had made the journey to the Yellowstone and back about 20 times. There is much about him in Maximilian, Travels of 1833, pub. 1843, *passim;* in Palliser, 1853, p. 82, etc.; and he will frequently come up again in Larpenteur's narrative.

[7] Mr. Kipp may have so called the one-season house he built in 1831, but Larpenteur means by Fort McKenzie the definitive post of that name of 1832.

By far the best account of Fort McKenzie I have seen, giving history, full description, etc., will be found in a paper penned by Mr. Alexander Culbertson for Audubon, at Fort Union, Aug. 7, 1843, and first published in Aud. and his Journs., by Miss M. R. Audubon, Dec., 1897, ii, pp. 188-195, preceded by extracts from Culbertson's journal at Fort McKenzie of June 13-26, 1834, *ibid.*, pp. 178-180. Maximilian also describes the fort in his Travels, ed. 1843, chap. xix, pp. 242, 243. His account of the battle there, which he witnessed Aug. 28. 1833, occupies chap. xx, pp. 273-277, and his folio pl. 42 is a stirring picture of the scene—one of the very finest works of art in all that magnificent series. Likewise, Mr. Culbertson furnished Audubon with an account of a

after those two forts were established, the Upper Missouri Department was formed, of which Mr. McKenzie was the agent. Berger received $800 per annum as interpreter for the Blackfeet.

Having done my best to post the reader on

fight which occurred at Fort McKenzie between the Assiniboines under Gauché and the Piegans who were at the fort, Aug. 28, "1834." The story is given in full in Aud. and his Journs., ii, 1897, pp. 133-136. There was fighting enough, I wot, in that vicinity—hardly a coulée unreddened with blood thereabouts; but probably not two battles on an Aug. 28. As the Maximilian date is certain, I suppose the Culbertson date of "1834" to be a mere error of transcription, and the two narratives to be of the identical engagement. Maximilian was at Fort McKenzie Aug. 9–Sept. 4, 1833. Compare also Larpenteur's story on p. 92.

The A. F. Co. had no permanent post among the Blackfeet, Piegans, Bloods, and Prairie Grosventres (Atsinas) till 1832, as it had been too dangerous to attempt to trade with those hostile and bloodthirsty Indians. Fort McKenzie was begun that year under the direction of David D. Mitchell, then a clerk A. F. Co., afterward U. S. Indian Agent; "the fort was completed by me, Alexander Culbertson, then a clerk of the Company, now [1843] one of the partners. During the first year, owing to the exigencies of the occasion, a temporary though substantial fort was erected. . . During the following year another fort was commenced and completed, and retained its former name of Fort McKenzie, being named after Kenneth McKenzie, Esq., one of the partners of the Company."

This establishment was often known as the Blackfoot post, Fort Brulé, and Fort Piegan or Piekann. It is repeatedly mentioned by the latter name in Maximilian's Travels. Thus, p. 239 of the English ed. of 1843: "Maria River, called, by the Canadians, Marayon; after we had passed it, we saw . . the ruins of the

these matters [of 1827-33], I resume my personal narrative. Yet a few words more in reference to the energy of Mr. McKenzie, who once remarked to me, in a conversation on In-

---

first fort or trading post, which Mr. Kipp, clerk of the American Fur Company, had built in the territory of the Blackfeet. This fort was abandoned in 1832, and the present Fort McKenzie built in its stead." Again, pp. 242, 243: "Fort McKenzie, which, at the time of its establishment, in 1832, was called by Mr. Mitchell, its founder, Fort Piekann, is designed for carrying on the fur trade with the three branches of the Blackfoot Indians, and several other neighboring nations, as the Gros Ventres des Prairies, the Sassis [Sarcees], and the Kutanas, or Kutnehas [Kootenays]. . . The American Fur Company concluded, in the year 1831, a commercial convention with those tribes, and sent for that purpose the interpreter, Berger, a Canadian. . . As soon as it was agreed to by both parties, Mr. Kipp was sent with a keel boat laden with goods to Maria River, and Fort Piekann, now [1833] in ruins, was founded. As the situation at the fort was subsequently found to be unfavorable, Major Mitchell, who succeeded Mr. Kipp, transferred the trading post to its present situation."

The definitive Fort McKenzie of 1833 was situated on the north or left bank of the Missouri, about 6 m. above the mouth of Maria's river; it stood 15 feet above the water and 225 feet from the bank of the river, on a piece of prairie a mile long, rising to hills half a mile in the rear; opposite the fort was a perpendicular bank of black clay, 150 feet high; the river was here 100 yards wide. It was a palisaded and bastioned structure, 200 feet square. During its whole existence it was the most important link in the chain of events which extended in space from the Yellowstone to above Maria's river, and in time from 1832 to the founding of Fort Benton in 1846.

dian trade, that his intention had been at that time to extend the trade into the Rocky Mountains; and that, not feeling disposed to do so without a charter, he made application to the government; but that ours being a free government, no charter could be allowed him, and thus the project was abandoned.

After the flogging of our gentlemen nothing special took place until a certain free trapper named Augustin Bourbonnais came down the Missouri in a canoe. As it was yet early, about the 1st of November [1836], his idea was to keep on to Fort Clark and winter there. But as he found many of his friends at Union, he changed his plans and made up his mind to spend the winter at this place. He had been lucky on his hunt, and had about a pack of beaver, worth something like $500, which made him feel rich and quite able to pass a pleasant winter. Bourbonnais was only about 20 years of age, a very handsome fellow, and one thing in his favor was his long yellow hair, so much admired by the female sex of this country. This they call pah-ha-zee-zee,[8] and one who is so adorned is sure to please them. A few days before his arrival Mr. McKenzie, who was nearly 50 years old, and perhaps thought it was too cold to sleep

[8] " Riggs' Dict. has : *Paha* = hair of the head, the scalp ; *zi*, yellow ; *zizi*, redundant of *zi*, yellow, *i. e.*, very yellow. Hence *pahazizi*, very yellow hair."—W. M.

alone in winter, had taken to himself a pretty young bedfellow. Mr. Bourbonnais had not been long in the fort before he went shopping, and very soon was seen strolling about the fort in a fine suit of clothes, as large as life, with his long pah-ha-zee-zee hanging down over his shoulders; if he had looked well in his buckskins, he surely looked charming then. Cupid, I suppose, commenced to shoot his arrows so fast that they struck Bourbonnais, unfortunately for himself, as they also had Mr. McKenzie; and as such arrows generally wound to the heart, Mr. McKenzie determined to go on the war path. Being somewhat advanced in age, he found he could not carry on the war with arrows; so he armed himself with a good-sized cudgel and watched his opportunity. It happened one evening that Mr. Bourbonnais, encouraged by favorable returns of affection, went so far as to enter the apartments reserved for Mr. McKenzie. The latter, hearing some noises which he thought he ought not to have heard, rushed in upon the lovers and made such a display of his sprig of a shillelah that Mr. Bourbonnais incontinently found his way not only out of the house but also out of the fort, with Mr. McKenzie after him. It was amusing to see the genteel Mr. Bourbonnais, in his fine suit of broadcloth, with the tail of his surtout stretched horizontally to its full extent; but, unfortunately for the poor fellow, he

would not let the affair end in that way, and swore
vengeance on Mr. McKenzie. Of course, having
been driven out of the fort with a club, he did not
think it proper or consistent with his dignity to attempt to enter again; so he took board and lodging
in an Indian tent, many of which were pitched near
the fort, and all his effects were delivered to him.
Then it was reported that Mr. McKenzie would be
killed; for, " kill him I must," Bourbonnais had said;
but, thinking that his angry passion would soon sub-
side, we made or thought little of the threat. Yet,
sure enough, he was seen next morning dressed again
in buckskin, with his rifle on his shoulder and pistol
in his belt, defying Mr. McKenzie to come out of the
fort and swearing that he would kill him if he had to
remain on the watch for him all winter. Still thinking that such performances would not last long, Mr.
McKenzie preferred to remain a day or so in the fort,
rather than have any further disturbance. But Bourbonnais kept up his guard longer than Mr. McKenzie
felt like remaining a prisoner in his besieged fort;
in consequence of which a council of all the clerks was
called with the view of raising the siege either by persuasion or by force, and so it was agreed that Bourbonnais' life was to be taken in case he could not be
induced to desist. As a measure of precaution a written instrument was immediately prepared and pre-

sented to the men of the fort, to sign if they thought proper, and they were particularly informed that the main object was to scare Bourbonnais away—as in reality it was. Next morning one of his friends was sent to him on the part of Mr. McKenzie, to notify him of what had taken place, and to advise him to leave; but that availed not, for he continued his hostile demonstrations. Having given him ample time to change his mind, and seeing that he did not budge, a mulatto named John Brazo [9]—a man of strong nerves and a

[9] Dr. Matthews kindly furnishes the following note : "There was a white Brazeau (John, I think) and a colored Brazeau on the Upper Missouri. It was the latter that I knew. He used to say he was the first 'white man' that ever came into the country. I think he came as a servant or slave to the former. My John Brazeau was a full-blooded Æthiopian, apparently, of small stature and intelligent, though not handsome, face. He must have been 70 or over when he died. He enunciated his English well and had a good command of it for an uneducated man. He spoke French better than most Canadians; also Sioux and other Indian languages. He was hardy, courageous, and on the whole a creditable specimen of his race. He served the A. F. Co. and its successors for many years. About 1868, the company he had been working for at Fort Berthold sold out to an opposition concern, which had houses outside the fort. The people of the latter firm moved in and turned all the old hands out, including Brazeau, who was now too old, feeble, and rheumatic to work. He was literally turned out to die ; no white man offered him anything. Then the Indians took pity on him and gave him such shelter and food as they could afford ; but they were, themselves, very poor at this time. Hearing of this I had him conveyed 14 miles to Fort Stevenson, where I was then serving.

brave fellow, who had on several occasions been employed to flog men at the flagstaff—was sent for and
asked if he thought he had nerve enough to shoot
Bourbonnais, in case he should be desired to do so.
To which he replied, "Yes, sir—plenty!" "Well,
will you do it?" "Yes, sir; I am ready at any time."
John was then ordered to take his rifle into one of the
bastions, and shoot when he got a chance. John, as
good as his word, took his position. I recollect that
it was early one Sunday morning, a little before sunrise, when Brazo came to my room, saying, "Mr.
Larpenteur, I have shot Bourbonnais." As none of
the men were up, I went to apprise Mr. McKenzie of
it, who said, "Has Brazo killed him?" Bourbonnais
had fallen, but it was not yet known whether he had
been killed or only wounded, and I was told to take
three or four men to see about it. Mr. E. T. Denig,
the bookkeeper, who understood some little surgery,
went with us. When we reached the spot we found
Bourbonnais only wounded and that not mortally,
the ball having struck him above the right breast, and
gone out through the right shoulder. He was then
brought into the men's quarters, where his wounds

My hospital being overcrowded, I furnished a shack near by for
his accommodation, and sent his meals to him. He was able to
sit up and talk, to the last. One morning, when the attendant
brought him his breakfast, Brazeau was found kneeling at the
side of his bed, dead."

were dressed by Mr. Denig, but it was not until the following spring that he was able to leave the fort. He remarked that when he was shot he was on his way to his canoe, at the mouth of the Yellowstone, with the intention of going down to Fort Clark. He left early in the spring and what became of him I never heard; as he was quite pale and not entirely cured when he left, it was thought he might die.

Now, gentle reader, that story is told, and next comes one concerning myself, which has nothing to do with Cupid's arrows, but something to say of those made and shot by Indians. That same spring, on the 1st of March [1837], an express arrived with the information that an individual named Millieu [Mileau?] was coming with a small outfit to trade with a band of Canoe [10] Assiniboines who generally remained in the neighborhood of White river, and requesting Mr. McKenzie to send a party from Fort Union to oppose him. I was pitched upon to go, and next day started down with a small

[10] For this tribe, and a classification and census of the Assiniboines, see Henry's Journ., 1897, pp. 522, 523, and my note there. He knew these people well, having been in business with them for some years, and his division of them into eleven bands is no doubt more reliable than that of Maximilian, who gives only eight: see also Fifteenth Ann. Rep. Bur. Ethnol., 1897, p. 161 of an article in which McGee identifies as Assiniboines the " Essanapes " of the mendacious or highly imaginative Baron La Hontan. They are the Assinipoualaks or Guerriers de Pierre of

outfit on three one-mule sleds.   These Canoes were
considered at that time the worst band of Assiniboines—great thieves and troublesome to the traders;
they seldom came to the fort and left it without com-
mitting depredations, and it had happened that they
stole several head of horses the previous fall.   As
liquor was the surest means to recover stolen horses,
I was provided with the article for that purpose, as
well as for another.   But as luck would have it, I was
prevented from reaching the Indian camp on this
trip, for at our first camp, which was at the Big
Muddy river, 24 miles below Union, a young Assiniboine appeared with a letter from Mr. McKenzie, requesting me to turn back, as Millieu had been killed
by the Sioux and there would be no opposition; besides which, the Indians had threatened to cut the
ears off my mules, and would be likely to rob me.
Early next morning we were on our way back to Fort
Union, which we reached in good time that day.

Having been quietly reinstated in my former func-

the Jesuit Relations of 1658, and are supposed to have separated
from the Wazikute gens of the Yanktonais Sioux before 1650,
when they became the Hohe or " Rebels."   The trouble seems
to have been due to the same thing that caused the Trojan War
and most other notable events in the history of the human race,
beginning with eviction from an original abode of peace—a
woman, *varium et mutabile semper*, as Vergil hath it, with fine
disregard of gender.

PIERRE GARREAU.   AUGUST, 1870.
(Died about 1881.)

tions, I thought no more of taking a tramp until another express brought the information that the Opposition had come up river and were already with the band of Canoes; and that Mr. D. D. Mitchell, the person in charge of Fort Clark, had sent a half-breed named Pierre Garreau [11] after them, but requested Mr. McKenzie in the meantime to send some

---

[11] " The Pierre Garreau whom I knew," says Dr. Matthews in a letter to me, " was the son or reputed son of a Frenchman or Franco-American.   This first Garreau was, I think, the ' Mr. Garrow' of Lewis and Clark.   The second Garreau, Pierre, was the Mis or Beesh of the Hidatsa Indians, whom in your ed. of L. and C., p. 245, you appear to have confounded with his father or reputed father.   Many of the old settlers said that my man was a full-blooded Arickaree, and only a stepson of the elder Garreau ; but I doubt this.   When you see his portrait, I think you will recognize Gallic features in it, though he was as dark as any Indian.   He had been taken to St. Louis in boyhood and taught the trade of baker.   He spoke French and several Indian languages fairly well, but Arickaree best (his mother was an Arickaree).   Although he was interpreter for many years at Fort Berthold, both for traders and the military, his command of English was not good.   When an important council was on hand he translated the Indian speech into French, and some Frenchman, who spoke better English, translated it to the Americans.   I once attended a council in which he was inter-preter, and the speech of the visiting Indians passed through four languages to reach us—Cheyenne, Arickaree, French, Eng-lish.   He was courteous in his manners, very intelligent, and was highly esteemed by all his associates, white and Indian.   When I knew him he had no children left ; all were dead.   Boller relates how three of his sons were killed by the Sioux.   Dr.

few goods, such as Garreau did not have. I was
called on again, and started next day with three dog-
sleds and some liquor, to recover the stolen horses if
possible.   The third day I arrived in camp, which was
then called the Tobacco Garden [12]; it was 100 miles by

W. J. Hoffman once showed me an excellent portrait of him
which I think belongs to the U. S. Bureau of Ethnology."
   Boller in his Among the Indians, 1858–66, pub. 1868, has much
to say of Pierre Garreau : special accounts of him at pp. 181, 182,
and of the killing of his three sons at one fell swoop of the Sioux,
pp. 245–248.   Boller considers him to have been a full-blooded
Arikara, whose widowed mother married the elder Garreau
before the birth of her son ; but nothing could have been simpler
than for the actual father to have become the step-father by
marriage.
   [11] Tobacco Garden creek was discovered by Lewis and Clark,
Apr. 17, 1805 ; it is the "little run from the north" of their
itinerary for that day, ed. 1893, p. 275.   It is an insignificant
tributary of the Missouri which falls into the left side of this river
in Williams Co., N. Dak., half-way between Big Muddy and
White Earth river, 39 m. (air line) below Fort Buford, say 50 by
the trail, and perhaps 75 by the channel of the Missouri.   It will
be found traced on any fairly good map of that region, mostly
without any lettering by name; but is easily identified as the
little stream crossed by the G. N. Ry. next W. of station Whee-
lock.   It is lettered "Reed Bottom" on Stevens' map, and the
same name appears on Twining's, but " Tobacco Garden " seems
to have been its most frequent, though erroneous, designation.   I
was there in June, 1874, with the U. S. Northern Boundary Survey ; in the Report of which, 1878, p. 75, Major Twining says :
" Owing to the slow progress made by the boat, I was obliged to
land the live stock at the Tobacco Garden, and herd it from that
point to Fort Buford, where it arrived on the 15th of June, a few

water from Union. Soon after my arrival I sent for the chiefs, and told them that the chief of the big fort had requested me to assemble them to assist me in recovering the stolen horses, and that I would make them a present of a little liquor. I then gave them each a pint of whiskey. Two of the horses were soon brought to me, for which I gave the Indians a small keg containing one gallon. For fear that those horses might be retaken, I mounted two good men upon them, and ordered them to put for the fort.

hours after the boat." That this name is a mistranslation of the Indian term appears from the following, kindly furnished by Dr. Matthews:

"When I first learned the Hidatsa name for the Tobacco Garden creek (meaning Place where the Reeds Grow) and found that other Indian names had the same meaning, I was surprised, and started inquiries. I was then told by Charles Paquenaud, and other well-informed men, that the name Tobacco Garden came thus: The Sioux and Assiniboine name for reed is *cedi* (cheddy) and the name for tobacco is *čandi* (chandee). Some early traveler who first bestowed the English name was confused by the resemblance of these words and mistranslated the Sioux. Where the creek enters the Missouri bottoms there is (or was in my day 1865-72) a wide marsh where common reeds (*Phragmites communis*) grew abundantly. I have had a modern guide point out to me 'the very spot where the Mexican found the plug of tobacco that he named the creek from,' and I have had another wiseacre show me the place 'where the old Indian planted the tobacco.' Of course, Indians cultivated a native tobacco (*Nicotiana quadrivalvis*) in those days; but not in separate gardens, apart from corn, etc."

There was an Indian by the name of Pet-cah-shah,[11] which is their word for Tortoise, who was known as the greatest scamp of this band; he was the son of their biggest chief, and the identical genius who had stolen the horses. The liquor trade meanwhile commenced. Mr. Tortoise got very drunk, and rushed into my lodge, saying, " You are the meanest white man I ever saw—you traded a lodge from me too cheap last fall—you would not give me the knife I asked you for." He went on enumerating his grievances and exclaimed, " I will kill you to-night!" We knew he was not a bit too good to do it, and soon heard him yelling in an awful manner. Suddenly he rushed into the lodge with his bow and arrows, and had it not been for a young Indian—a friend of mine —who had time to draw his knife and cut the bow string, very likely I should not now be writing. After this performance he came up to me holding a handful of arrows with which he punched me in the breast, saying, " You dog of a white man, I will kill you yet!" He rushed out again and was soon seen with a short Indian gun cocked, but it was taken out of his hands by main force and the priming removed. Then he went to the fire, from which he took out some large smoldering chunks of wood and commenced to rub

[11] Or Patkasha, which is a better spelling of the word.

his dirty head with them, making the live coals fly in all parts of the lodge, as though he intended to set it afire. I don't believe Old Nick himself could have cut a worse figure in his infernal regions. But he was plainly getting too drunk for this sort of thing to last; after cutting a few more capers he rushed out again, and this was the last we saw of him that night.

Soon after that another and still uglier-looking devil of an Indian made his appearance, rushing about in the same manner. This was Hooting Owl, upward of six feet tall, blind in one eye, naked but for his breech-clout, painted in a most hideous manner, and with a long scalper in his hand. Standing immediately before us, he commenced to talk at a great rate, and was apparently very angry; but what he meant by his remarks I could not understand, as I was not well acquainted with the language. But from his postures and gestures I made sure we were gone up this time. To strengthen me in this belief he began to tear up the ground with his long knife, like a furious bull; then, without saying another word, rushed out of the lodge. I asked Garreau what this meant, to which he replied that the Indian was all right; he had only been saying that he had just heard how we had been treated by the Tortoise, and that he intended to cut up the first Indian who should trouble us again, just as he had cut up the ground. This was good news, and I thought that if I were to adopt a bird as an emblem, I would take the hooting owl in preference to the eagle.   I had already made away with the liquor on the sly, as the Indians would not let me do so publicly; the noise subsided and finally ceased, and thus the frolic ended.

Next morning some chiefs and big men came to express their regret that I had been so badly treated, and everything went on quite smoothly; but Mr. Pet-cah-shah never showed himself again.   My orders being not to remain more than three days, and not knowing the way back from this camp to the Big Muddy, but wishing to make the fort the same day—a distance of 40 miles—I hired an Indian as guide.   When I told him that I intended to reach the fort that day he remarked that I could not do it; that we would have to travel at night, which was impossible, on account of the prickly pears.   Seeing him determined to turn back when we had come in sight of Big Muddy, and knowing the road myself from that river to the fort, I agreed to let him go.   I sat down, took out my pocket book, and drew him an order for what he was to receive for his trouble, as Garreau could neither read nor write.   Although I was not much of a draughtsman he understood the picture very well when I was through with the drawing, which indicated a looking-glass, a number of hawk-bells, a knife, a pallet of vermilion, and a piece of scarlet cloth in the shape of a breech-clout—though this last I had to explain to him. After he had got this and smoked his pipe we separated, and about eleven o'clock at night I entered Fort Union with my feet nearly frozen. As this was the end of March, and it had thawed all day, the river bottom was all water; but at sundown the wind changed to the northwest, the water commenced to freeze, and when I got to the fort my moccasins were so hard frozen that I had to let them thaw before I could get them off. Had there been an hour longer to travel, my feet would surely have been frozen.

Thus ended my first introduction to an Indian camp. Hoping that I should never have another occasion, I went to bed and slept soundly; but it will be seen in the sequel that I was frustrated in my hopes, if my reader will have the patience to read this book through. As I have to go on with my stories in rotation, it will be some time before I again take him to trade whiskey in an Indian camp.

After my return from the Canoe camp nothing worthy of remark took place until the arrival of the steamer, late in June [1837].[14] The mirth usual on

[14] It is highly satisfactory to find that we have kept Larpenteur's chronology quite correct to this point. It is true that 1838 was the great smallpox year, as given by De Smet, Catlin, and

such occasions was not of long duration, for immediately on the landing of the boat we learned that smallpox was on board.   Mr. J. Halsey, the gentleman who was to take charge this summer, had the disease, of which several of the hands had died; but it had subsided, and this was the only case on board. Our only apprehensions were that the disease might spread among the Indians, for Mr. Halsey had been vaccinated, and soon recovered.   Prompt measures were adopted to prevent an epidemic.   As we had no vaccine matter we decided to inoculate with the smallpox itself; and after the systems of those who were to be inoculated had been prepared according

many other writers; we are now at the beginning of the epidemic in 1837.   The Orig. Journ. has a long special article on the subject, dated Fort Union, Aug. 13, 1837, and opening thus: "Remarkable Events of the Small Pox brought to this Post by the Steam Boat Saint Peter on the 24th June 1837." This fixes the date precisely, and the Autobiography is now seen to have run in regular sequence of events narrated—what Larpenteur above calls "in rotation"—from 1833 to 1837.

It appears from the Orig. Journ. that Mr. Halsey's case was followed by that of Mr. Denig, both ending favorably. Meanwhile occurred a fatal case of a lying-in woman, and after the alarm had become general 17 persons were inoculated on July 12.   Among those who died Larpenteur names Baptiste Contois, a half-breed, and adds: "During his illness some more were expected to Dy sure Enough on the 4 Day of August my Squaw expired, . . . and on the 12 the Poor Contois Was Put in to his earthley Dwelling."

to Dr. Thomas' medical book, the operation was performed upon about 30 Indian squaws and a few
white men. This was done with the view to have it
all over and everything cleaned up before any Indians
should come in, on their fall trade, which commenced
early in September. The smallpox matter should
have been taken from a very healthy person; but, unfortunately, Mr. Halsey was not sound, and the operation proved fatal to most of our patients. About 15
days afterward there was such a stench in the fort that
it could be smelt at the distance of 300 yards. It was
awful—the scene in the fort, where some went crazy,
and others were half eaten up by maggots before they
died; yet, singular to say, not a single bad expression
was ever uttered by a sick Indian. Many died, and
those who recovered were so much disfigured that
one could scarcely recognize them. While the epidemic was at its height a party of about 40 Indians
came in, not exactly on a trade, but more on a begging visit, under the celebrated old chief Co-han; and
the word was, " Hurry up! Open the door! " which
had been locked for many days, to keep the crazy
folks in. Nothing else would do—we must open the
door; but on showing him a little boy who had not
recovered, and whose face was still one solid scab, by
holding him above the pickets, the Indians finally concluded to leave. Not long afterward we learned

that more than one-half of the party had died—some
said all of them. In the course of time the fort became clear of the smallpox, but the danger of infec-
tion continued. Fort William [15] was still standing,
and the remaining houses, which were no longer inhabited, were used as hospitals for Indians, with no
other attendants than some old squaws. It became
the duty of John Brazo to take out the dead and dump
them into the bushes, and some mornings, on asking
him " How many? " he would say, " Only three, sir;
but, according to appearances in the hospital, I think
I shall have a full load to-morrow or next day." This
seemed to be fun for Brazo, but was not for others,
particularly myself, as I happened to be the trader,
who was liable to be shot at any time; but, singular to
say, not even a threat was made, though the tribe was
reduced more than one-half by next spring [1838].
Trade continued very nearly up to the average: on
being asked how it happened that there were so many
robes brought in, the Indians would say laughingly
that they expected to die soon, and wanted to have

[15] The original one of that name having been eradicated and
transplanted alongside Union, as we have seen, p. 72; "the remaining houses" being those not burned during the Deschamps
massacre of June 28–29, 1836, p. 100. Larpenteur keeps the name
in double employ, sometimes for the original site of Fort William,
and sometimes for the buildings which were removed from that
place to another position.

a frolic till the end came. The winter [of 1837-38] was spent in great suspense and fear, but, fortunately, nothing serious occurred except some few shots fired at me through the wicket during the night liquor trade; and as this had frequently happened before, it was not attributed to revenge for the smallpox.

CHAPTER VIII.

(1838.)

ROUND TRIP TO THE STATES.

IT happened that this was an open winter; the ice broke up early in March, and the river was clear on the 22d of that month, at which date I left for Baltimore in a small canoe, with Mr. Robert Christy of St. Louis. He had come up in the fall to winter at Fort Union for his health, and becoming anxious to return, had made up his mind to leave, in spite of all the dangers represented to him. On my part, I had not seen my parents for ten years, and as this early start would give me ample time to visit them, until our party should be ready to return in the fall, nothing could persuade me out of the notion. Mr. D. D. Mitchell, a member of the Company, and very much of a gentleman, got me to engage for another year, previous to my departure, allowing my wages to run on during my absence; so this trip was considered as a furlough.

Matters being thus well fixed Mr. Christy and I left, with two men to row our canoe.

The day was calm and beautiful; and we made good speed. I was young, and full of mirth at the idea of returning to my parents, whom I intended to take by surprise, and many other fine plans I had formed made me so happy that I forgot the danger of Indians. Suddenly a party of them, who had concealed themselves along the river banks, rose up with their bows and arrows, ready to shoot. We were not more than 20 yards from them, and their work of destruction would have been quickly done had it not been for one among them whom we saw running to and fro with his bow in his hand, striking right and left. He finally succeeded in preventing the threatened attack; and, as one can imagine, the progress of our little craft was speedily increased. We were told, on our return, by Mr. Chardon,[1] a member of the Company in charge of Fort Clark, that we had no idea how near we came to losing our lives on that occasion. Those Indians

[1] François A. Chardon was a well-known man in the business, whose name frequently occurs in books of trade and travel on the Missouri. He was in charge of Fort McKenzie in 1842, when, with Alexander Harvey and others, he became infamous for the Blackfoot massacre described beyond, and next year built Fort Chardon above the mouth of the Judith. He was in charge of Fort Berthold Apr. 1, 1848, when Palliser reached that post, p. 197, but was already very ill, and his death occurred that spring or summer, as noted by Palliser, p. 263.

were a party of 80 Rees [Arikaras], who had gone to war on the Assiniboines; and had it not been for their partisan's great influence over them we surely would have all been killed. The Rees had had the smallpox severely, and were therefore badly disposed toward the whites. This was fright No. 1, after which I remember well the first words spoken by Mr. Christy: "Larpenteur, I think we had better stayed at Union." But it was already too late to repent; we were under way and could not turn back.

At ten o'clock of the second day after this, when we were near Heart[2] river, on the south side of the Missouri, we discovered six Indians, who had gone hunting while the ice was still strong; but it had broken up before their return, and now they had no means of crossing the river. Thinking this a good opportunity to save themselves the trouble of making their own boat, they made signs to us to come for them. These Indians belonged to the band of Canoe Assiniboines, who had had the smallpox badly, and whom I had known to accept pay for being ferried over the river, instead of paying us for the privilege; so of course I declined the job. As soon as

[2] Some slip here. Heart river is nearly opposite Bismarck, N. Dak., which is much below the Mandans, where was situated Fort Clark; and Larpenteur is still far above the latter. Perhaps he meant to say Little Missouri river.

they saw our craft steered away from them, they threw off their robes, and, with nothing on but their leggings and breech-clouts, ran to head us off. This they were near doing, as we had to go close to the shore to avoid the waves caused by the strong current washing against sand bars. As we approached they seated themselves, steadied their guns with the ramrods to take good aim, and let fly at us. But by this time we had got a little ahead of them, rowing all the time with all our might, though we could see the flashes from the muzzles of their guns and hear the bullets strike the water. Mr. Christy, who was steering, dodged like a duck passing under a bridge, to avoid the balls which whistled about his ears. We soon got out of their reach, but this danger was not the worst that appeared. The Indian camp was only a little way off, and, having heard the firing, they were all on the alert, thinking we were enemies. They soon found out the cause of the firing, and ran down to the next bend with the intention of giving us another volley. They fired at us again, but, fortunately for us, the river was wide, the current free from waves, and we could keep our distance from the shore. Bullets fell on the water like hail, some even beyond us, and three of them lodged in our canoe. These we afterward extracted with our knives. At length, finding ourselves out of danger, and also out of breath after having paddled with all our might through two attacks, those who had pipes began to smoke, and jocose remarks were made in regard to our scare. Some said, "This is fright No. 2; I wonder what No. 3 is going to be? It cannot fail to happen, as we have already had two in so short a distance, and the third time we must surely go up!" I began to feel like agreeing with Christy, that we had better have remained at Union.

After the pipes were emptied, the paddles were again plied, and our little wounded craft slid down stream gently. We kept on in a pleasant manner until next day, at about eleven o'clock, when we discovered a large number of Indians on the south side of the river, running back and forth and gathering on a small hill quite near the bank. Their maneuvers appearing hostile to us, we knew not what to do, and began to fear we were surely gone up this time. It was thought best to land on the opposite shore, to decide upon what course to adopt, and it was left optional with each one to take it by land or water. Not feeling like footing it, I went in for the boat; and after a little further parley, seeing me determined to do so, they all agreed to follow my example. So I placed a good supply of tobacco on the bow of the canoe, in full sight, to produce a good effect, if possible, and on we started. When they saw us coming they increased in number and our fears rose in proportion; but keep on we must. When our fears were at the highest pitch we perceived an individual with pants and a red flannel shirt on, looking very much like a white man. To our surprise and joy, we found that it was old Mr. Charbonneau,[3] who had been 40 years among the Missouri Indians. He used to say that when he first came on the river it was so small that he could straddle it. Imagine our joy to find our-

[3] Toussaint Charbonneau, Lewis and Clark's interpreter of 1805-6, who was engaged at the Mandans to accompany the expedition to the Pacific, and whose wife, Sacajawea the Bird Woman, rendered important service as guide and in other ways: See L. and C., ed. 1893, pp. 189, 224, 244, 257, etc. Larpenteur's " 40 years " would bring Charbonneau to the Missouri in 1798, which is no doubt about right; he is not heard of much after 1838, but I have found no record of his death. History is silent regarding the death of the lowly heroine Sacajawea, who should never be forgotten as the guide of the L. and C. expedition at some of its most critical junctures, as when she pointed the way out of Ross' Hole to Captain Clark, July 6, 1806, over the Continental Divide by Clark's (or Gibbon's) Pass, ed. 1893. p. 1122; and again, July 14, when she is praised by him for piloting him over Bozeman Pass to the Yellowstone, p. 1132. Dr. Matthews explains to me that there should certainly be no sound of j in her name. The word is composed of *Tsakáka* or *Sakága* = bird + *wía* = woman —the g very hard, and the whole accented Saka'ga-wi'a. This should be remembered when the time comes, as I hope it may, for a monument to stand on the summit of one of the passes here said, in commemoration of signal services rendered to the United States Government by a slave Indian woman who was sold by her captors to Toussaint Charbonneau.

selves befriended instead of butchered, as we had thought we were surely going to be. The tobacco was presented to such Indians as the old gentleman advised, and we resumed our paddles.

Charbonneau told us that we were then something like 70 miles from Fort Clark,[*] but thought that we

---

[*] See Lewis and Clark, ed. of 1893, p. 179. This was the post at the Mandans, for the trade of these Indians and the Grosventres, and long one of the most noted establishments on the river. The most satisfactory account I have seen may be read in Maximilian's Travels of 1833. The book is rare in this country; I have seen but two perfect copies, both of these of the English ed. of 1843, 4to text, with folio atlas of magnificent plates. One of these copies formerly belonged to John James Audubon, bears his autograph, and is now owned by his granddaughter, Miss M. R. Audubon, at Salem, N. Y. The prince has much to say of Fort Clark, as on pp. 318, 319, etc., 323, etc., and gives a diagram of the location on p. 394. It appears that James Kipp, a Canadian of German descent, came to the place as agent of the Columbia F. Co. in 1822, when there was no post. Major Pilcher, who came up the Missouri with Maximilian in 1833, to take charge of Cabanné's Omaha post, and was in 1822 a proprietor of the Missouri F. Co., directed a post to be built a little above the Minnitaree villages, on the S. side of the river. This was abandoned in 1823, when the Mo. F. Co. was dissolved. In May, 1822, Mr. Kipp began a fort on the prairie which lay between the future Fort Clark and "the forest in which the inhabitants of Mih-Tutta-Hang-Cush live in the winter." This structure was completed in Nov., 1822. In Nov., 1825, Mr. Kipp went to White Earth river, where he built a fort a little below its mouth, and wintered 1825-26, trading with the Assiniboines. In the winter of 1830–31 Mr. Kipp caused wood to be prepared for a new fort, and the palisades were erected in the spring of 1831. Mr. D. D.

would be detained by the ice, as frequently happened, this being about the most northern point on the Missouri. Gladdened again, fright No. 3 being over, and fairly under way, we traveled well the balance of that day. The next day we found but little current, and had to paddle hard to make much headway. We went on thus until about three in the afternoon, when we found the river nearly blocked by large dykes, which had formed across it and caused the slowness of the current; but we forced our way through a narrow channel, and kept on by hard paddling. By the time we were about 10 miles from Fort Clark the

Mitchell then undertook the direction of this new post, which he completed to some extent and named Fort Clark. In July, 1831, Mr. Kipp was sent to Maria's river, where he built the first Fort Piegan and wintered 1831–32, when he was succeeded by Mr. Mitchell, who began to build the later Fort Piegan or McKenzie (completed by Mr. Culbertson). Thereupon Mr. Kipp returned to Fort Clark, where he wintered 1832–33 as clerk under Mr. Lamont, and then took charge in 1833. Fort Clark was about ¾ m. below the old Fort Mandan of Lewis and Clark, and on the other side of the river, 300 paces from the Mandan village above said, 80–90 paces from the S. bank of the Missouri, 200 paces above a streamlet which receives a branch at 200 paces from the fort, after issuing from the hills back of the level piece of prairie on which the fort was built. About a league below Fort Clark was a wooded bend of the Missouri, where was the winter location of 60–70 huts to which Maximilian refers, belonging to the Mandans of the first or lowest village, called Matootooha or Matootonka by Lewis and Clark, ed. 1893, p. 182 ; but I understand that the above is a better spelling of the name.

dyke broke loose and the ice came down upon us with such a rush, and tossing our canoe like an old log at such a rate, that we thought ourselves in greater danger of our lives than we had been from the Indians; but at last it brought our canoe of its accord to shore about a mile above the fort, where we were obliged to remain two days till the ice subsided. Mr. F. A. Chardon, who was then in charge, and a very singular kind of a man, entertained us in the best manner. Mr. Christy had a two-gallon keg of good whiskey, of which Mr. Chardon was so fond that he helped himself about every fifteen minutes, saying he had " a great many worms in his throat "—to the sorrow of Mr. Christy, who found his keg so nearly empty that he concluded to make Mr. Chardon a present of what was left. We remained there two days; on the third we took leave of Mr. Chardon who, not knowing he was to fall heir to the balance of the whiskey, and not having as yet destroyed all the worms in his throat, would have been glad for us to remain another day, and insisted very strongly that we should do so. I cannot say whether it was because the whiskey had been put on board before Mr. Christy made up his mind about it, that Mr. Chardon accompanied us to the boat, or whether he did so through politeness; but he felt very happy at the presentation, and hastened back to the fort in double-quick time.

All right and off again; and I am glad to say that, with the exception of high winds, which at times kept us, for three days together, camped in the willows, nothing took place worth mentioning till we reached the Vermilion post.[5] Mr. Dickson, who shortly afterward committed suicide, was in charge, and showed us great kindness during the night we stayed with him. After relating to him our narrow escapes, he remarked that we were now out of danger, being among a different kind of Indians. This information sounded pleasant.

After a good breakfast next morning we left the kind Mr. Dickson, who, it appeared, did not quite know his Indians; for we had not made more than 20 miles when a volley of rifle-shots was fired at us by a deer-hunting party of Omahas. Fortunately we happened to be in a wide part of the river. The attack was so sudden that we had no time for fright before it was over; but, after this, we came to the conclusion that we could not consider ourselves safe until we reached the States. In constant dread of Indians, we kept paddling on our way, trusting to good luck to

---

[5] Fort Vermilion, so called from the well-known river of that name at whose mouth is now Vermilion, seat of Clay Co., S. Dak. But " the Vermilion post " was not exactly at this point: see a note beyond, in which I discuss the situation, at the date when Larpenteur takes charge of an establishment by this name.

get out of the Indian country; it was a long way to travel, as there was no settlement at that time on the Missouri above Independence, Mo. Our provisions were getting low, and altogether we were not in very good humor. On reaching the mouth of the Platte we perceived a steamer; and as but one steamer a year came that far up, we made sure it was the Company's boat. Our hearts were glad, expecting to hear all the news and procure a supply of eatables. We were soon on board the Antelope [6]—that being her name. Mr. McKenzie, who was on his way to Fort Union, was much surprised to see me. Said he, " My God! Larpenteur, what's the matter? Why have you come down so early in the season? " After learning the circumstances and being assured that all was right above, he became reconciled, and told me that he had been to my father's, in Baltimore, and had left them all well: " but go on," said he, " they will be very glad to see you." After a little more talk, we continued down river, well supplied with provisions and in a very good humor, though we had still a long distance to paddle. A few days after leaving the

[6] A boat of this name, but I should suppose not the one here in mention, was burnt 5 m. below Upper Bonhomme isl., Apr. 12, 1869. She was a side-wheeler, 180×32 ft., 326 tons, in the Benton trade, W. R. Massie, owner; total loss, boat $20,000, cargo $38,-000; chambermaid burned to death. (Chittenden, App. WW Ann. Rep. Chf. Engs., 1897, p. 3872.)

steamer we reached a small town called Camden,[1] where we met a boat bound for Fort Leavenworth, and made arrangements for our passage to St. Louis on her return, which we awaited at this little town. Having no further use for our little craft, we made a present of it to our two men, and next day we were comfortably lodged on board the steamer, whose name I have forgotten, as well as that of the captain. Great was the change, after paddling our own canoe for a month through all kinds of dangers, to find ourselves seated at table and gliding down stream at the rate of 20 miles an hour. At that rate it was not many days before we reached St. Louis.

I left next day for Baltimore by stage to Louisville, thence to Cincinnati, thence to Brownsville; then stage again to Baltimore. But at that time the stage stopped at Frederickstown [8]—I believe 40 miles from Baltimore—where we took cars which were propelled by horse power, not having as yet any engine.

As it is mostly my object to relate what happened in the Indian country. I will merely state here that I had great pleasure in seeing my relatives again, after the absence of 10 years; and as nothing was spared to make my stay agreeable, I enjoyed myself very much.

[1] Camden, Ray Co., Mo.

[8] Doubtless meaning Frederick. Md., which is 61 m. by rail from Baltimore.

Leaving the reader to imagine the surprise of my unexpected return, I will soon take him with me on the
way back to Fort Union. But, before starting up the
Missouri, I will give a little incident of my return to
St. Louis. This took place in a small town in the
Alleghany mountains called McConnelltown,[9] and
will show how one may get praised without deserv-
ing it, as happened to be my case. Mr. Denig, the
bookkeeper of Fort Union, whose parents resided in
this town, had given me a letter of introduction to his
father, the doctor, and also a letter of his own to his
parents, both of which I delivered with pleasure, as
the place was on the stage route. There was great
rejoicing on my arrival at Dr. Denig's. The old gentleman was about fifty and the old lady not far from
it; both were good, respectable people, who paid
all the attention to me that could be expected. I remained three days, during which a report was circulated that there was, at the doctor's, a certain gentleman who was said to be a crack shot. So a target
was prepared for a shooting match. Although I did
not consider myself a marksman, and, in reality, was
not, I accepted the challenge. There was no bet-
ting—it was merely to try me as a sharpshooter.
Their best marksman was picked out—one that could

[9] McConnellstown is in Huntingdon Co., Pa. It may be a question of McConnellsburg, Fulton Co.

knock out a squirrel's eye on the top of the highest
tree in the mountains at every pop. Accompanied
by the two sons of Dr. Denig, and two hired men,
we started for the appointed place, where a large
crowd of all sorts of people was awaiting my arrival,
with targets all ready for action. The conditions
were best three out of five shots at thirty paces, unless the center was driven. My opponent was a stout,
fine-looking Pennsylvania Dutchman named Keizer.
It was my first shot, and I made a close one; he shot
nearly a tie; but out of the five I happened to have
the best three. The target was taken down and
handed to me, and another immediately put up. It
was my first shot again, close to the black on the right
side; Keizer shot next, on the left, somewhat nearer
than mine. Then came my second shot, when I remarked, by way of braggadocio, being far from expecting to make good my boast, " Now, gentlemen,
this is what I like! When there is a shot on each side
of the black, it serves as a guide to me, and I generally drive the center." As much to my own surprise
as to that of all the rest, it was driven—so well that
this could not have been more precisely done by
hand. Imagine the looks in that crowd, disappointed to see their crack man so badly beaten!
But Keizer said it was owing to his having chased his
sheep that day, which made him so nervous that he

could not shoot.   I put both targets in my pocket-book, and brought them to Mr. Denig at Union. Old Dr. Denig was well pleased, and said, "Were I in your place, now that your name is up, I would not shoot any more."   Neither did I.

Next day I left McConnellstown, and nothing took place worth mentioning on the journey to St. Louis until our departure thence for Fort Union.   I should have said before that I left Baltimore on the 13th of September [?], 1838.   Mr. D. D. Mitchell, who had come down in the steamer, and was about to return to Union, was our chief; besides whom, Clerk Jacques Bruguière, myself, and two men composed the party. We traveled on pleasantly until we reached Poncah creek,[10] when most of our men were taken with fever and ague at such a rate that, instead of eating down they were all throwing up.   This kept us two or three days longer than we should have stayed at the creek. The day we left to strike for White Earth river[11] I

[10] Ponka or Ponca river, next above the Niobrara, on the same side of the Missouri, near the southern border of S. Dak.   See L. and C., ed. 1893, p. 108.

[11] The same which Larpenteur elsewhere and usually calls White river, the first considerable tributary of the Missouri from the N. above Little Knife river, in N. Dak.; station White Earth on it, where the railroad now crosses.   This is not the stream so called by Lewis and Clark (see ed. of 1893, pp. 275, 278), nor the White river of S. Dak.

was taken with such an awful shake that, when on
horseback, I could keep my seat only by holding on
with all my might to my rifle across my saddle; and
I cut such a figure that it excited the mirth of the
party, who laughed at me all through their pretended
sympathy. After the shake came the fever, and then
thirst—but no water—I thought I should die for want
of water. I had two such shakes before we arrived
at Fort Pierre, where we remained two days. Mr.
Halsey gave me some good medicine, and after a couple of light shakes I recovered entirely. Then came
the tremendous appetite. I was really ashamed of
myself at meal time. But Mr. Mitchell was very
liberal in helping us to well-filled plates, and when he
saw that I had made away with the contents of mine,
would say, " Back up your cart, Larpenteur, for another load." Only those who have traveled the prairie know what a voracious appetite is acquired on
such tramps. Having had the ague, which is always
followed by an increase of the regular prairie appetite,
we became ravenous, and soon made away with our
provisions. Three days before our arrival at Fort
Clark, at the Mandans, we were out of everything except sugar and coffee: for, singular to say, even at
that early period buffalo had become scarce.

Thus far I had proved myself to be about the best
hunter in the company, having killed some few ante-

lopes, badgers, and prairie-dogs, as we had been all
this time in the open prairies. When we were approaching Fort Clark, and had reached the points of
timber of the Missouri, I proposed to Mr. Mitchell to
try my luck in search of deer, as our rations had given
out and we had but one cup of coffee left. He readily
consented, saying, " Take Brazo along; he is somewhat of a hunter." Having been told where he would
camp, I and my man started together; but we soon
separated, each choosing his own direction through
the wooded point. I soon perceived a fine large buck.
I knew that my old horse would stand fire—you
might shoot off the whole of the United States artillery around him without making him move—standing still was his forte. I rose in my stirrups and
pulled the trigger; but away went the buck, not without leaving a lock of his hair, which I saw fly. Being sure that I had made a good shot, I got off my
steady old horse and commenced the search. In
the meantime Brazo, who had heard the shot, came
up and asked what I had fired at. I replied, " A large
buck, which I am sure I wounded." So he joined
me in the search; but, as I could find no blood, I soon
proposed to abandon the trail. Brazo then remarked, " No, Mr. Larpenteur, I have seen blood; let
us look a little while longer." Encouraged by this
we resumed our search, and in less than ten minutes

we saw the fine buck, stretched dead, having been shot through the heart. In a little while he was cut up and put on my horse, and we were on our way to camp. Brazo, not liking the idea of coming into camp without any game, struck out to try his luck again. I did not expect to get any more game on the way to camp; but luckily came full on a band of five deer, which stood about 80 paces from me. I drew a bead on one of them, which fell at the crack of the gun. No need looking for this one, as it was shot through the neck. Poor Brazo, who had got but a little way off, came up to ask what I had killed. I told him " A fine fat doe." " Well, you are in luck! " said he. Having cut up the meat and loaded it on Brazo's horse, we struck for camp, which we reached just at dark. I leave the reader to imagine the exclamations of joy made at the sight of so much fine meat; but the question arose, " Who killed all that? " I said I had killed both deer. Then it was " Hurrah for Larpenteur! Come, boys, get up your kettles! " While the kettles were boiling French voyageur songs resounded, and all felt quite set up except poor Brazo, who seemed to be down in the dumps.

The third day we entered Fort Clark early and found Mr. Chardon in charge, who received us with hoisted flag and several rounds from his small piece of artillery. There we took supplies to last us to

Union, and the following morning resumed our journey, Mr. Mitchell being our boss and guide. It was now October and the mornings were getting quite cold, with heavy white frosts. The second morning after we left Fort Clark my old horse tumbled into a miry little creek,[12] and, not being able to extricate himself, came down broadside before I could jump out of the saddle. When they saw me so well drenched they could not refrain from indulging in mirth at my misfortune. Our guide, not being very well scienced, struck too far south, in consequence of which we were three nights without wood and had to burn buffalo chips; but, as good luck would have it, we were favored with clear, dry weather and could make good fires. But our animals fared badly, as the route we took brought us into alkali country: some we had to leave, and others died at the fort.

On the fifth day after we left Fort Clark we struck White river, too far up; but we got into some scrawly timber, which was mighty good after having nothing but buffalo chips to burn for three nights. Brazo, who was in the habit of coming into camp last, said he had heard dogs barking, and also thought he had

[12] Doubtless Miry creek of Lewis and Clark, ed. 1893, p. 261, translating Rivière Bourbeuse of the French. This is present Snake creek, next above Wolf creek, and is a small stream from the right, which was crossed near its mouth by the regular trail from Fort Clark to Fort Stevenson.

heard squaws talking, and added, " There's Indians
close by." This news put a stop to our pleasant feelings and a guard was set. Apprehending attack
early in the morning, sleep was light that night; but
we happened to be mistaken in our apprehensions.
Daylight came all right, breakfast was gotten up, and
still no Indians; so we commenced to think Brazo had
been mistaken. But we had not left camp more than
an hour when some one cried out, "Indians!" Before
any preparations could be made, a whole host was
upon us; but we soon found that they were some
Assiniboines who had camped a little above where we
did last night; it was only on account of our late arrival that they had not discovered us. They told us it
would take us two more days to get to Fort Union,
for our horses were poor and we could not travel fast.
Some of the leading men proposed to go along with
us, which was agreed upon; for the sake of a little
whiskey they would have gone any distance. But
some of the rabble followed, whose looks we did not
like, and whom we would have been glad to see turn
back; for they looked very much like those who made
it a habit to borrow, and forget to return, a white
man's horse. As they excited great suspicion, the
guard was doubled; but, in spite of all our precautions, they managed to get off with two horses, one
of which belonged to an individual by the name of

Antoine Frenier, a half-breed whom Mr. Mitchell had engaged at Fort Clark as interpreter for Fort Union. When he found that his favorite horse had been borrowed and was not likely to be returned, he began to give the Assiniboines such a blessing, with the aid of the Virgin Mary, whom he invoked to assist him in strengthening his remarks, that I defy any Catholic priest to make a better one.   The Indians, who had learned by this time that he was to be the interpreter, were convinced, by this blessing, that he understood their language.   In spite of all this we were under way by sunrise, with glad hearts after all, thinking that we had but once more to sleep outside, excepting the old interpreter, who now and then addressed a prayer to the Holy Virgin for the benefit of the Assiniboines, and to the great mirth of the company, sometimes in French and sometimes in Assiniboine, but always mixed with a little Cree, as he was a half-breed from the North.   It seemed impossible for him to recover from the loss of his nag sufficiently to abstain from his devotions.

Our last camp was on the Big Muddy.[13]   Although we hoped that we had gotten rid of the horse thieves,

[13] Present name; last considerable stream from the N. below the mouth of the Yellowstone; Williston at its mouth, where the railroad crosses. This is the White Earth river of Lewis and Clark, ed. of 1893, p. 278, but not the White Earth or White river of present nomenclature.

it was thought proper to keep up a strong guard, which consisted of one-half of the party for each half of the night; but as it was very dark, the Assiniboines made out to take two of our best horses, one of which was Mr. Mitchell's. The chiefs said that they knew who had stolen the horses, and told us not to be uneasy, for we should get the animals back again. They proved as good as their word; our two horses were returned shortly afterward, though the interpreter's was never recovered. Thus, half consoled, we again got under way, and did not stop until we entered Fort Union, which we did about 4 p. m., with a salute of many shots from the artillery, and the large flag flying. This was on the 12th of October [1838];[14] and my reader can guess who felt good after a six-weeks' ride through the wild prairies.

[14] The year 1838 is correct, but Larpenteur is out at least a month if, as he says on p. 150, he left Baltimore Sept. 13; he could not have gone from Baltimore to Fort Union inside of a month. He has been traveling in such good weather that most probably the Baltimore date is wrong, and the Fort Union date right.

CHAPTER IX.

(1838-42.)

COMPOSED OF ALL SORTS.

THANKS to kind Providence, here I am again in good old Fort Union, at a splendid table, with that great prairie appetite to do it justice. The day after my arrival I was reinstated in the liquor shop, and as it was the height of the meat trade I had enough to do, night and day. Excepting plenty of buffalo, deer, and rabbit hunting, nothing took place worth mentioning until Christmas [1838]. On this anniversary a great dinner is generally made, but that was never the case here, as it was always taken out in drinkables instead of eatables; and I, who did not drink, had to do without my dinner. At the height of the spree the tailor and one of the carpenters had a fight in the shop, while others took theirs outside, and toward evening I was informed that Marseillais, our hunter, had been killed and thrown into the fireplace. We immediately ran in, and, sure enough, there he was, badly burned and senseless, but not dead yet. We were not at first sure whether this was the mere effect of liquor, or had happened from fighting; but we learned that a fight had taken place, and on examination we found that he had been stabbed in several places with a small dirk. Knowing that the tailor had such a weapon, we suspected him and demanded it. He was at that time standing behind his table; I saw him jerk the dirk out of his pocket and throw it under the table. I immediately picked it up; it was bloody, and from its size we judged it to be the weapon with which the wounds had been inflicted. Having learned that the carpenter had also been in the fight, they both were placed in irons and confined to await their trial. As such Christmas frolics could not be brought to a head much under three days, the trial took place on the fourth day, when a regular court was held. Everything being ready, the criminals were sent for, the witnesses were well examined, and after a short session the jury returned a verdict, " Guilty of murder." The judge then pronounced sentence on the convicted murderers, which was that they be hanged by the neck, until they were " dead, dead, dead! " But, not considering it entirely safe to have this sentence executed, he changed it to thirty-nine lashes apiece. John Brazo was appointed executioner. Always ready for such sport, he immediately went in quest of his large ox-whip, and, not making any difference between men and oxen, he applied it at such a rate that Mr. Mitchell, the judge, had now and then to say, " Moderate, John, moderate "; for had John been suffered to keep on, it is very likely that the first sentence would have been executed.

After this everything went on perfectly smooth. A very large trade was made, and everybody was satisfied; and in time preparations were made to take down the returns.   On the 3d of June [1839] I was sent to St. Louis in charge of eight Mackinaw boats, each containing 250 packs of buffalo robes, besides many small furs.   The trip was very pleasant, with the exception of being nearly shot by Assiniboines at the same place where we had been attacked the previous spring.   The disagreeable features of these trips are caused, mainly, by the crews getting whiskey and becoming unruly; but I managed to get along admirably well, and succeeded in landing all my boats safe in the port of St. Louis.   These were the last landed there, as no companies would insure below St. Joseph, on account of the drunkenness of the men, which had caused the loss of many boats.

For what reason I have never been able to find out, though I always attributed it to that old tyrant, Mr. Laidlaw, the Company would not then hire me again; so I remained that winter [of 1839-40] in St.

Louis. It happened during this time that Mr. Mc-
Kenzie, Mr. Mitchell, and old Mr. Chabané [1] got at
difference with the American Fur Co., in consequence
of which they raised a large outfit to oppose it; but
by some means the misunderstanding was made up.

In the meantime I had been re-engaged, and arrangements were made for my return to Fort Union.
On the 31st of March [1840] I was on the steamer
Trapper, and after a long, tedious trip we reached
Union on the 27th of June. My being a sober man
was not much to my advantage, keeping me constantly in the liquor trade, and out of the charge of

[1] John P. Cabanné. The surname appears in many forms; if
one of these be Cabanis, it is that of at least two celebrated
European scientists—Pierre Jean George Cabanis, the French
physicist and psychist, and Dr. Jean Cabanis, the German orni-
thologist. But as to the great fur trader, John P. Cabanné of
St. Louis: "On May 1, 1813, 'Berthold & Chouteau' opened
their new firm. . . This was the foundation and origin of what
in a very few years thereafter, by the addition of two new partners, Messrs. Jno. P. Cabanné and Bernard Pratte, Sr., . . . became the great and wealthy ' American Fur Company,'" Billon,
Ann. St. Louis, 1804-1821, pub. 1888, p. 234. In the same Annals,
pp. 399-402, is a biographical sketch of J. P. Cabanné, with plate
of his country homestead of 1819; his later city residence, built
1833, was No. 20 Vine St., St. Louis, where he died on Sunday,
June 27, 1841, aged 68 years, having been born in France, Oct.
18, 1773. His wife was Julia Gratiot, b. July 24, 1782, m. Apr. 8,
1799, d. Apr. 14, 1852; they had eleven children, among them
John Charles Cabanné, b. Nov. 4, 1806, d. July 17, 1854, whose
eldest son was John Pierre Cabanné, jr.

posts which some of my fellow-clerks took charge of,
while I did all the work, and was really in charge
when they got dead drunk.   Mr. Laidlaw the Father,
Mr. Denig the Son, and Mr. Jacques Bruguière the
Holy Ghost, formed the Trinity at Union last [?] winter, and a trio of greater drunkards could not have
been got together.   The consequence was that the
large meat trade was lost.   Indians would trade robes
with Mr. Laidlaw in the office, steal them back, and
trade them again with Mr. Bruguière at the regular
shop.   The reason why Mr. Laidlaw opened trade in
the office was, he said, that Bruguière got too drunk
to hold out; but Laidlaw was the greater drunkard
of the two.

About the latter part of May, 1842,[2] Mr. Alexander
Culbertson, who was in charge of Union, sent me up
to Fort Van Buren, at the mouth of Rosebud river,
on the Yellowstone, with a party of 10 men, to bring
down the returns.   He also instructed me to build
another post at Adams Prairie, about 20 miles above,
where he expected me to remain in charge, as he was
not sure that Mr. Murray, who was then in charge of
Van Buren, would be re-engaged.   Next day we left

[2] So copy, distinctly written out—"It was in forty-two, about
the latter part of May."   I have no Orig. Journ. by which to
check dates along here, but that 1842 is correct will appear by
the De Smet incident, etc., beyond.   Larpenteur has nothing for
1841 except what is given in the preceding paragraph.

Union, and a pleasant trip we had. Our guide, a young man by the name of Lee, who was a first-rate hunter, made us live on buffalo tongues and marrow bones. A few days after my arrival at Van Buren the boats were off with the returns, and I remained in charge of my first post.

Nothing of importance occurred during the time I remained at this place except one little incident, which I think deserves a place in this narrative.[3] Two or

[3] Audubon tells the same story, June 28, 1843, Journ. ii, 1897, p. 65—doubtless he had it from Larpenteur himself: "One of the engagés of the Company was forced to run away, having killed an Indian woman, and made his way to the Crow Fort, 300 miles up the Yellowstone. When he arrived there he was in sad plight, having his own squaw and one or two children along, who had all suffered greatly with hunger, thirst, and exposure. They were received at the fort, but in a short time, less than a week afterwards, he again ran off with his family, and on foot. The discovery was soon made, and two men were sent after him; but he eluded their vigilance by keeping close in ravines, etc. The men returned, and two others with an Indian were despatched on a second search, and after much travel saw the man and his family on an island, where he had taken refuge from his pursuers. The Buffalo-hide canoe in which he had attempted to cross the river was upset, and it was with difficulty that he saved his wife and children. They were now unable to escape, and when talking as to the best way to return to the fort, the soldiers saw him walk to the body of a dead Buffalo lying on the shore of the island, with the evident intention of procuring some of it for food. As he stooped to cut off a portion, to his utter horror he saw a small Grizzly Bear crawl out from the carcase. It attacked him fiercely, and so suddenly that he was unable to de-

three weeks after the boat left, a certain Mexican, who had been employed at Fort Union, made his appearance with his squaw nearly naked, and said to me, " Mr. Larpenteur, I will tell you the truth.   I killed a squaw at the meat camp.   I did not intend to kill her; but she made me mad.   I took a stick, struck her on the back of the head, and she fell dead. I then ran off, fearing some of her connections, who were in camp.   That is the whole truth, captain "— as he called me.   " Now I am very poor," he continued, " and my India "—as he called his squaw—" is going to have a child.   Will you please let me go into your fort?   I will do anything you want me to do." Having but four men with me, all told, and seeing the Mexican so pitiable, I allowed him to come in. Mexicans being only fit to herd horses, I employed him on horse-guard.   Had his India not been with him and so near confinement, I would not have given him that employment.   For a while he did very well, being attentive to his duties, and all were pleased with him.   One fine afternoon he came to me, saying, " My horses are all doing well.   I have got them in a

fend himself; the Bear lacerated his face, arms, and the upper part of his body in a frightful manner, and would have killed him, had not the Indian raised his gun and fired at the Bear, wounding him severely, while a second shot killed him.   The engagé was too much hurt to make further effort to escape, and one of the Company's boats passing soon after, he and his family were taken back to the fort, where he was kept to await his trial."

good safe place. Will you be so kind as to let me go with my India in search of some pomme blanche?" which is the French name for Indian turnips [*Psoralea esculenta*]. As he had done so well and his India was so near her time, I consented, and off he started, assuring me that he would not be gone more than a couple of hours. But that time passed, and neither the Mexican nor his India appeared; and some of the men said they should not wonder if he had made his escape. This being the general impression, they examined a little old box in which he kept his duds and found it empty. I immediately sent after the horses, which we supposed he had mounted, but found them all right. Next morning, knowing the situation of his squaw, and thinking that he might be lurking around for a chance to steal horses, I sent my hunter and an old Crow in search of the Mexican, under promise of $10 reward if they should find him. About 3 p. m. I saw them returning; the old Indian having the squaw behind him on his horse, with the child in her arms, and the Mexican trotting behind with nothing on but his shirt—thus all ready to be tied up to the flagstaff. This was immediately done, and he would have received a good dose, had not he begged so hard and looked so pitiable that he was let go unpunished. They had found him about 10 miles below the fort on the banks of the Yellowstone, where he had made a raft to cross over; but the raft, not being well constructed, came apart when in the middle of the river, and he lost all his duds except his shirt in saving his squaw, who, he said, had her child immediately on landing, the fright having hurried the birth. I pitied the squaw, but the Mexican I determined to ship off. So the next morning I gave him a skin boat, a little dried buffalo meat, a knife, a steel for striking fire, and a fish-hook and line, with which I told him to clear out and never make his appearance at this place again.

Not long after this occurrence Mr. Auguste Chouteau arrived with the outfit for the Crows, also bringing back the Mexican and his lady. On reprimanding him for so doing, he told me that he could not well help it, considering the situation in which he had found them. It had happened that the Mexican, on his way down river, saw a buffalo mired near the bank; and, having no meat, thought this would be a good opportunity to lay in a supply. Judge of his surprise when Mr. Bruin, who was lying in wait behind the buffalo, made a grab at the man, tearing him so badly that, when he was met by Mr. Chouteau, he was scarcely expected to live. Thus ends the story of the Mexican, except that, some time afterward, he was killed by the relations of the squaw he had murdered at Union.

Among the news that Mr. Chouteau brought up was that of Alexander Harvey's killing Isidoro, the Spaniard.   As I shall have frequent occasion to mention Harvey, I will here give some idea of his character.   He was a native of St. Louis, who served some time learning the saddle trade with Thornton Grimsley.[4]   As he happened to be one of those men that never can be convinced, and with whom it was no use to argue unless one wished to get into a fight, he remained but a short time at his trade.   Though not yet of age he engaged with a fur-trapping company for the Rocky Mountains.   Having found his way to the mouth of the Yellowstone about the time that Fort McKenzie was built, he engaged with the American Fur Company for that post.   There he remained for a number of years [to fall of 1839]; but became so wicked and troublesome, and was so much feared by all hands at the fort, that reports were made to Mr. Chouteau in St. Louis, who sent him his discharge by the fall express, which did not reach Fort McKenzie until about Christmas.   He was undoubtedly the boldest man that was ever on the Missouri —I mean in the Indian country; a man about six feet tall, weighing 160 or 170 pounds, and inclined to do right when sober.   On hearing of his discharge,

[4] Thornton Grimsley and Wm. Stark had a harness shop in St. Louis, Aug. 20, 1820.   (Advt. in a newspaper of that date.)

and being requested to report in person at St. Louis
—which was simply to get him out of the country—
he remarked, " I will not let Mr. Chouteau wait long
on me. I shall start in the morning; all I want for my
journey is my rifle, and my dog to carry bedding."
Sure enough, in spite of all remonstrances regarding the hardships to which he would expose himself
on such a long journey alone at that season of the
year, he set out, good as his word.

Early in March he reached St. Louis, to the great
astonishment of Mr. Chouteau, who, after hearing
Harvey's story, and learning what a journey he had
performed, could not but re-engage him to return to
Fort McKenzie. He returned at the same time that
I reached Union, in the steamer Trapper [June 27.
1840]. On the way up he now and then remarked to
me, " Larpenteur, I have several settlements to make
with those gentlemen who caused me last winter's
tramp; I never forget or forgive; it may not be for
ten years, but they all will have to catch it." Being
as good as his word, at Fort Clark he pounded
awfully one of the men who had reported him, saying,
" That's No. 1." On his arrival at Fort Union,
where many had come down with the returns, intending to go back with the outfit to Fort McKenzie, and
never thinking of coming in contact with Harvey,
they were much surprised when he made his appear-

ance among about 60 men, in search of reporters; and at every glimpse he could get of one of them it was a knockdown, followed by a good pounding. Whiskey had nothing to do with this; he was perfectly sober, only fulfilling his promises. This will show what sort of a man Harvey was; but there is more to tell, and now we return to the Spaniard story.

It was in 1841, when the Spaniard and Harvey happened to go down together with the returns, which were then taken in Mackinaw boats to St. Louis. Both intended to return in the steamer, which they expected to meet below Fort Pierre. The report was generally believed, though I placed no reliance on it, that a plot had been laid on the way up to Union, by some members of the American Fur Company, for the Spaniard to kill Harvey. Both had long been stationed at Fort McKenzie, but had never agreed, being jealous of each other and great enemies. The next day after the departure of the steamer—a day given to the men to look about and arrange their little effects—the Spaniard took occasion to commence hostilities, and was soon parading with his rifle, saying that he would kill Harvey. For the first time in his life Harvey was persuaded to remain in the house, supposing it was only liquor that caused the Spaniard to make those threats; so the day passed, and Harvey was still alive. The second day, all the clerks

were called up to get the equipments ready for Fort
McKenzie. Mr. Culbertson, who was in charge of
Union, came into the warehouse; not seeing the
Spaniard with the other clerks, he asked where the
man was, and, being told, sent for him. But Isidoro,
instead of going to the warehouse, went into the retail store and remained behind the counter. Mr.
Culbertson and Harvey both being in the store, Harvey began by asking the Spaniard what he meant by
his behavior the day before. " You are too big a
coward to come out and fight me like a man; you
want to shoot me behind my back!" So saying, he
left the store and dared the Spaniard to come out;
but the latter never moved. When Harvey found
that his enemy would not come out, he went back in
the store and said, " You won't fight me like a man,
so take that!" and shot him through the head.
After this he went to the middle of the fort, saying,
" I, Alexander Harvey, have killed the Spaniard. If
there are any of his friends who want to take it up,
let them come on "; but no one dared to do so, and
this was the last of the Spaniard.

Now we will set fire to Fort Van Buren, according
to instructions, and proceed to erect Fort Alexander,
which I named in honor of Mr. Alexander Culbertson.

Having burned Fort Van Buren,[5] I left with 20

[5] The Journal of Lieutenant James H. Bradley appears in the
Cont. Mont. Hist. Soc. ii, 1896, pp. 140-228. This is one of the

laboring men for Adams Prairie, 20 miles above by land, about 40 by water.   With the exception of having my horses stolen by Assiniboines on two occasions, and going on a bear hunt with Indians, which latter incident I will narrate, nothing took place at Van Buren worth mentioning.   The theft of the horses put me to a great deal of trouble, and was a great

most readable things one could wish to see, giving a lively, realistic account of the Sioux campaign of 1876 under General John Gibbon, and showing that history as well as literature lost a man of much promise in Bradley's death.   The campaign he portrays with such fidelity culminated in the Custer massacre—just where Bradley's narrative breaks off.   He was killed at the battle of the Big Hole in the Nez Percé campaign, Aug. 9, 1877, while gallantly leading his company (B) of the 7th U. S. Infantry in a charge on Chief Joseph's camp.   General Gibbon was an old army friend of mine; I well remember an evening he spent at my house in Washington in 1893, looking over Lewis and Clark's MSS., discussing Clark's or Gibbon's Pass on the Continental Divide, and then the battle of the Big Hole, in which the gallant old soldier was badly wounded, besides being, as he said, "licked like the devil" by Joseph, whom he characterized as one of the best soldiers and most thorough gentlemen he had ever known.   But the saddest incident of the fight, he seemed to think, was the death of Lieutenant Bradley.   Not long after that the impressive spectacle of General Gibbon's funeral was seen in Washington—but that is another story. . .

Bradley says, pp. 198, 199: " Another object of my visit to the mouth of the Rosebud was to inspect the ruins of the old trading fort that once stood here.   It bore the name of Fort Van Buren and was built by Tullock in 1839, to replace Fort Cass situated

drawback in the building of the new fort.   One fine
evening, early in September [1842], a certain Crow
returned from searching for his horses, saying that
a Mr. Grizzly was breakfasting on one of them, and
that, as one man was not enough to make the bear
let go his prey, he came for assistance.   A bear being
considered by Indians a more dangerous enemy than

just below the mouth of the Big Horn and abandoned the previous year.   It was the second post maintained by the American
Fur Co. on the Yellowstone, and had enjoyed an existence of
only three years when it gave way to Fort Alexander, built by
Larpenteur, in 1842, on Adams' prairie, some twenty miles
higher up the Yellowstone.   The accounts of the fort represent
it as having been a little over a hundred feet square, and I judge
from the remains, though I made no measurement, that it was.
Seven ruined stone chimneys and a slight ridge where the palisades stood are all that is left of it.

" I recorded in my original journal of this visit: ' The palisades
must have been burned, as the ridge is marked with cinders and
ashes;' and by an old manuscript that has fallen into my hands I
find that it was, Larpenteur having set fire to it himself on the
completion of his other fort.   The fort stood on a plateau some
eighteen or twenty feet above the present level of the water, a
few yards from the bank of the Yellowstone, and about seventy-
five below the delta of the Rosebud."

By our present account it appears that Larpenteur fired Fort
Van Buren before he built Fort Alexander.   But this is a small
matter to adjust in comparison with the difficulty of reconciling
such conflicting statements regarding Van Buren as I have criti-
cised on p. 47, unless there were two places of that name at
different dates and on widely separated sites.   It is no wonder
that Bradley is at one with Larpenteur regarding the Rosebud

a man, a good force was raised, and I, wishing to see
the fun, volunteered to go with them. We soon
came to the spot, where we saw Bruin lying fast asleep
behind the remains of his breakfast. Knowing that
Indians considered it braver to strike an enemy after
he had been shot down, than to shoot him down, I
was prepared to be very brave. When we were within 30 steps, one of the Indians made a little noise, at

site of Van Buren, because the " old manuscript " above said is
the one we are now printing, Dr. Matthews having loaned it to
him.

Rosebud river falls into the right side of the Yellowstone from
the S., between stations Rosebud and Albright of the N. P. R. R.,
and late U. S. General Land Office maps mark " Old Fort Alexander" here. Now this appears to be an error; for Fort Van
Buren was the one at the mouth of this river, and Larpenteur
tells us he built Fort Alexander higher up, at Adams prairie. I
regret that my Lewis and Clark reflects this mistake, saying that
Fort Alexander was " at or near " the mouth of the Rosebud, p.
1159, where *read* Fort Van Buren. I passed both these old sites
Sept. 14, 1893, but was thinking of something else at the time,
and made no observations upon them, in my haste to inspect
Clark's autograph inscription on Pompey's Pillar.

Fort Sarpy, also at the mouth of the Rosebud, 1850-55, is said
to have been the last A. F. Co. post on the Yellowstone. The
present military establishment is Fort Keogh, near Miles City
and the mouth of Tongue river. This was a new and nameless
cantonment in 1877, whence Gen. N. A. Miles made the swift and
spirited dash which resulted in the final surrender of the splendid
Nez Percé chieftain on Eagle creek, in the Bear Paw mountains,
after he had been chased by Gen. Howard for more than 1300
miles. A modern Moses, in sight of the Promised Land !

which the bear awoke and rose up to see who were the intruders. A volley was fired; the bear dropped dead behind his breastworks, and we all counted coups upon his carcass with our ramrods, I among the first.

Soon after that Mr. Chouteau returned from St. Louis to Fort Union, having gone down with Father De Smet,[8] who was on his way from the Columbia to the States. His most important news was that a strong Opposition had arrived; the firm was Fox, Livingston and Co. of New York. They had come up in a steamer, with a large outfit, and were building a Mackinaw boat for the Crows' trade of the Yellowstone; so that we should have opposition here. This

[8] Peter John De Smet, the Belgian Jesuit priest, noted for his extensive travels and missionary labors among the Indians, and still more so on account of the several books he wrote about them, one of which has already been cited in another connection. The mention of Father De Smet is fortunate, as it enables us to fix the date—1842: see Oreg. Missions, 1847, p. 39, where it appears that in 1842 "Father De Smet was bending his steps back to St. Louis, to procure additional laborers for the mission." The next spring, on May 1, 1843, Audubon overtook him on his upward journey : see Aud. and his Journs., i, 1897, p. 467: "When we reached Glasgow, we came in under the stern of the 'John Auld.' As I saw several officers of the United States army I bowed to them, and as they all knew that I was bound towards the mighty Rocky Mountains, they not only returned my salutations, but came on board, as well as Father De Smet."

news I did not relish; for opposition is necessarily a great nuisance.

In the meantime the work on Fort Alexander was progressing finely; my men were good hands, determined to put up a well-built little fort, which was very near completion by the 15th of November [1842]. I was already in my quarters, very comfortably located, thinking that I was going to pass a pleasant winter with my family. Like all other traders I had taken a better half,[7] who had made me the father of my first child on the 9th of last August. But all these fine expectations were ended by the unexpected arrival of Mr. Murray,[8] who had been engaged to take charge of Fort Alexander, with letters from Mr. Culbertson requesting me to return immediately to Fort Union, where I was wanted mighty bad in the liquor department. This was not the first time I had found out that being a sober man was no advantage to me.

I left next day with one man and two horses—one

[7] His second wife, the first having died at Fort Union in 1837: see note [7], p. 132. Dr. Matthews tells me that all the children of this alliance died before their father—the last of them, Elizabeth, of consumption, at Fort Buford, at 10.45 p. m., Feb. 26, 1871.

[8] The same who has been already incidentally mentioned, p. 162. I once made the following memorandum from Palliser, 1853, p. 83: "Mr. Murray, a Scotchman in the service of the [American Fur] Company, and in charge of Fort Alexander on the Yellowstone," where Palliser met him in 1847.

to ride and one to pack.   As it was cold, and snow
on the ground, I had to leave my better half behind.
One of our horses soon gave out, and our trip of
eight days was a tough one.

I should remark here that, about two weeks before
I left Fort Alexander, a gentleman by the name of
Frederick Groscloud arrived in charge of a Mackinaw boat, with a fine equipment.   He had been formerly in the employ of Mr. Tulloch, and understood
the Crow language, but was not considered a person
of much force of character.

CHAPTER X.

(1843-44.)

WINTERING AT WOODY MOUNTAIN.

ABOUT the 1st of December, 1842,[1] I made my entrance again in Fort Union. It was at night; a large trading party were at the highest pitch of drunkenness; boss and clerks not far behind them in this respect. But I did not find it strange or surprising. Mr. Culbertson, on seeing me, remarked, " Well, Larpenteur, I am mighty glad to see you. We are having a hot time, and I'm tired of it. I suppose you are tired, too, and want to go to sleep." I supposed that he, having drunk so much, did not think about eating, for I had not got that invitation as yet, so I replied, " I'm not so tired as I am hungry." " Well," said he, " there's plenty to eat." I ran to the kitchen, and the cook got me up a rousing supper. I ate too much, and next morning found myself foundered;

[1] Copy has " 1841"—clearly a mistake of Larpenteur's memory, which I correct. See adjustment of dates in notes to last chapter.

but I had received orders to resume the grog department, and, notwithstanding my stiffness, went on to
set things in order.   They needed it very much.

In the course of time [2] I was informed of the cause
of this appointment.   A certain individual by the
name of Ebbitt had, a year previous, brought up a
small equipment and made his way as far as the Sioux
district.   He had a small Mackinaw with 12 men,
which was considered by the American Fur Company too slight an affair to oppose; in consequence
of which he made a very profitable return of 500

---

[2] " In the course of time " covers a considerable portion of 1843,
during all of which year Larpenteur was at Fort Union.   In taking up his MS. I expected of course to find mention of Audubon's visit to Union in the summer of 1843, with which I had
familiarized myself in reading his Journals, before their publication by Miss M. R. Audubon (New York, Charles Scribner's Sons,
Dec., 1897).   His party, consisting of himself, Edward Harris, John
G. Bell, Isaac Sprague, and Lewis Squires, reached Fort Union on
the steamer Omega, Capt. John A. Sire, at 7 p. m. of Monday,
June 12, and left in the Mackinaw boat Union at noon of Wednesday, Aug. 16, 1843.   It probably did not occur to Larpenteur
that one of these visitors was the most distinguished person who
had ever come to see him; or, if he had any such idea, it left no
impression on his mind; for he never mentions one of them by
name, nor does he even note their arrival or departure.   On the
contrary, Audubon repeatedly speaks of Larpenteur: see Journs.
ii, pp. 41, 65, 68, 73, 77, 81, 124, 126, 183, at dates running June
19–Aug. 8.   In a special article on Fort Union, by Mr. Edwin T.
Denig, at date of July 30, 1843, Larpenteur is named as being
then in charge of the retail store.

packs of robes. Elated with his success he went to New York with his returns, and there formed an acquaintance with the great firm of Fox, Livingston and Co.,[3] telling them how cheaply he had traded, and also remarking that the American Fur Company so abused the Indians and clerks that everything was working against them—in fact, if a large company, such as would inspire confidence among whites and Indians, should be organized. the American Fur Company would soon leave the country. This story took well; such a company was formed, and started in charge of a gentleman by the name of Kelsey, one of the members of the new firm. Mr. Kelsey had not ascended the Missouri very far before he began to regret what he had done, which was that he had put $20,000 into the concern. The farther he came up river the more he regretted it; and when he arrived at the mouth of the Yellowstone and saw Fort Union in its full splendor, he could not refrain from remarking to Mr. Culbertson, " Had I known how the American Fur Company were situated, I would have kept clear of investing in this opposition "; and concluded by saying, " I hope you will not be too hard on

[3] Audubon, when approaching the Great Bend, May 25, 1843, speaks of meeting three Mackinaws belonging " to the (so called) Opposition Company of C. Bolton, Fox, Livingstone & Co., of New York," Journ. i, 1897, p. 511. This was the second year of the Company, which first came up in 1842.

us." The old gentleman went off, leaving a man
named Cotton in charge. Mr. Kelsey, who, according to agreement, was to remain in the Indian country and make his headquarters among the Sioux,
chose a point * 20 miles below Fort Pierre, opposite
a beautiful island. Upon this there were four men
living in a small cabin, which he considered his. He
ordered them several times to leave; but they paid no
attention to him, and remained in possession. One
morning the old gentleman armed himself and determined to make the men leave. On entering the

---

* Fort George, which was built on the S. (right) side of the
Missouri, on a small creek of the same name, at the 1156¼ mile
point of the river by the Mo. R. Commission chart of 1882, which
marks Rousseau's ranch on the same creek, in the Lower Brulé
Sioux Reservation, S. Dak. The site in mention was 3½ m. below
the mouth of Little Medicine creek, which falls in on the opposite (left) side of the Missouri; this is the Wiyo Paha Wakan or
East Medicine Knoll river of Nicollet, Warren, and Raynolds,
originally Reuben's creek of Lewis and Clark, ed. 1893, p. 127 ;
Rousseau, P. O., Hughes Co., S. Dak., at its mouth.

That this is the very spot Larpenteur means is confirmed by
the narrative of Audubon, who reached Fort George at 3 p. m.
Sunday, May 28, 1843, and says, Journ. i, 1897, p. 519: " This is
what is called the ' Station of the Opposition line;' some Indians
and a few lodges are on the edge of the prairie. Sundry bales of
Buffalo robes were brought on board, and Major Hamilton, who
is now acting Indian agent here until the return of Major Crisp
[?Dripps] came on board also. . . He pointed out to us the
cabin on the opposite shore, where a partner of the ' Opposition
line' shot at and killed two white men and wounded two others,

cabin he fired at one of them, who was in the act of taking a kettle off the fire, and who fell dead in the fire. Another one, who ran out, was also shot, and fell dead over the fence. By that time a third man, who was trying to escape in double-quick time, was shot through the shoulder, of which wound he came near losing his life. During the following night the old gentleman made his escape. I was informed that he went to Mexico. This was the last of Mr. Kelsey.

Mr. Cotton, the person left in charge at Fort William, which he now called Fort Mortimer,[6] had not yet

all of whom were remarkable miscreants." This is obviously the same incident that Larpenteur relates in greater detail. In the same connection Audubon repeatedly mentions a Mr. Cutting, as "a young gentleman," etc. Larpenteur's "Cotton" and Audubon's "Cutting" are the same person, though which is the right name I do not know. Audubon says on p. 524, "Mr. Cutting was writing to his post near Fort Union to expect us, and to afford us all possible assistance." Compare also "Collins," next note.

I may mention here that alongside *old* Fort Pierre (the first one, 3 m. above Teton river), there was once a post called Fort Tecumseh, which had been abandoned and was in ruins in 1833: Maximilian, ed. of 1843, p. 155, where is also named a Fort Teton, of the French Fur Co., a little above Teton river, abandoned when the companies joined and old Fort Pierre was built.

5 As I have remarked in an earlier note, p. 52, Audubon has much to say of Fort Mortimer as it was in 1843. Visiting that post on June 23, he describes it as follows in his Journ. ii, p. 53: "We found the place in a most miserable condition, and about to be carried away by the falling in of the banks on account of the great rise of water in the Yellowstone, that has actually dammed

got dry—he was still green cotton, full of Mr. Ebbitt's stories about the general discontentment of Indians and whites. He soon commenced to try his hand on one of the most important chiefs of the tribe, Crazy Bear,[6] who, like many others, on learning that a big Opposition had arrived, came in with his band to pay them a visit. Mr. Cotton invited him into his room,

the Missouri. The current ran directly across, and the banks gave way at such a rate that the men had been obliged already to tear up the front of the fort and remove it to the rear. To-morrow they are to remove the houses themselves, should they stand the coming night, which appeared to me somewhat dubious." Again, July 1, p. 70: "Mr. Culbertson and I walked to the Pilot Knob with a spy-glass, to look at the present condition of Fort Mortimer. This afternoon Squires, Provost, and I walked there, and were kindly received as usual. We found all the people encamped two hundred yards from the river, as they had been obliged to move from the tumbling fort during the rain of last night." On July 13 Audubon went to Fort Mortimer to ask Mr. Collins, a young man from Hopkinsville, Ky., who was then in charge, to let him have a hunter named Boucherville to go after mountain sheep, p. 86. This man Boucherville was a famous hunter and trapper; Palliser, p. 198, met him at Fort Berthold in April, 1846, took him into his service, and has much to say of him in his book, *passim*.

[6] Assiniboine name Mato Witko, in French L'Ours Fou. This chief was one of the deputation which accompanied Father De Smet to a great council in 1851. A letter from him appears in De Smet's Western Missions and Missionaries, New York, 1859, pp. 130–132. No doubt it reflects the savage's statements and sentiments fairly enough, but the language has been fancifully dressed in translating it into English for publication. Crazy Bear first met De Smet at Fort Union, in the summer of 1851.

made him a great speech, dressed him up in a splendid military suit, such as had never been brought into the country before, and then laid a two-gallon keg of whiskey at his feet. Crazy Bear's band was at Union, waiting for his return; but, instead of going directly to them, he went into Mr. Culbertson's private room, not very drunk, took a seat, and remained some time without saying a word. Mr. Culbertson, surprised to see him so splendidly dressed, and thinking that he had lost his chief, was also silent. Finally Crazy Bear broke the ice by saying, " I suppose you think I have left our big house. No; I am not a child. I went below to see the chief, who treated me well. I did not ask him for anything. I did not refuse his presents. But these cannot make me abandon this house, where are buried the remains of our fathers, whose tracks are yet fresh in all the paths leading to this place. No, I will not abandon this house!" After which he rose from his seat and took off his fine fur hat and feathers, which he threw on the floor with all his might; then unbuckled his beautiful sword, with which he did the same; and kept on till he had stripped himself of all his fine clothes, without speaking a word. When this performance was over he said to Mr. Culbertson, who stood in great astonishment, " Take away all these things and give me such as you see fit, and don't think I am a child who can be seduced with trinkets." This Crazy Bear, who was not at all crazy, proved afterward to be the greatest chief of the Assiniboines.

Mr. Cotton, on hearing of this, was so surprised he could scarcely believe it; but when Mr. Culbertson showed him the suit, which had been badly torn, he was convinced, and began to think that Mr. Ebbitt's stories had been somewhat exaggerated. That was the way the green cotton commenced to dry. Still, his trade was pushed to the extreme. He had plenty of goods and was very liberal with them. Both sides then began to send out men to the Indian camps; but as all the most important camps were soon supplied, I began to think that I might escape that disagreeable trade. Being always an unlucky man, I was still disappointed in this.

One evening toward the last of January [1844], while I was thinking of anything but that which was forthcoming, Mr. Culbertson sent for me to come to his room. It was extremely cold and a great deal of snow was on the ground. This, I believe, was the reason he did not broach the subject at once, but finally said, " Larpenteur, I want you to go to Woody Mountain,⁷ to a camp of Crees and Chippewas, who

⁷ Woody Mountain recalls to mind my own experiences on the U. S. Northern Boundary Survey, season of 1874, when, starting from Fort Buford, June 21, I was in a few days camped at Fort

have plenty of robes, and have sent for traders from both companies. The Assiniboines have also sent for traders at the meat-pen, which is on the same road that you are going. I want you and Mr. Denig to go into the store, get up your equipment to-night, and start in the morning." Such were my orders, at short notice, after thinking I was going to remain at the fort. I had to make a trip of at least 100 miles, northward into the British possessions, and this was not calculated to make me feel very good. But Mr. Denig and I went to work, and at midnight the equipments were ready. Next morning with one sled apiece, two mules and one driver to each sled, we started on our journey, accompanied by several In-

M. J. Turnay, on Frenchman's river, near the parallel of 49° N. Woody Mountain is a long, irregular mass of drift, making a series of elevations—some of them up to 3,800 feet—which straggle E. and W., mainly between long. 106° and 107° W., 10 to 20 or more miles N. of the British boundary. From their N. slopes the drainage is by Woody Mountain river in the watershed of the South Saskatchewan; on our side these elevations give rise to both the main branches of Poplar river, tributary to the Missouri below the mouth of Milk river, and to the heads of Little Rocky creek, which falls into Milk river next below the mouth of Frenchman's river. On the British side, Woody Mountain post occupies tp. 4 of range iii. W. of the 3d init. merid., in Assiniboia; the cattle quarantine is on the line of 49°, among the heads of Little Rocky creek, occupying tps. 1 of ranges v. and vi. A cart trail from the Red River of the North reaches Woody Mountain settlement, continuing thence to Fort Turnay, and so on to Fort Peck, on the Missouri above the mouth of Milk river.

dians, among whom was one called Wounded Leg, chief of the band of the Rocks, whose camp was at the sand hills, about 60 miles on our road from the fort to Woody Mountain.

At our first camp my interpreter, a half-breed named Andrew, was taken sick; he complained of headache, and in the morning he was so ill that I had to let him go back to the fort. I understood some little Cree, and, as many of them spoke Assiniboine, I thought I could do without him. Next day we reached Wounded Leg's camp, and took a night's lodging with him. My friend Denig had been for the past few days in such a state that it was impossible for him to freeze—he was too full of alcohol. He had not walked one step; this disgusted the chief, who proved an enemy afterward. The morning was so stormy that we would not have left camp had we not learned that the Opposition had gone by with dog-sleds. Not wishing to be outdone by them, I awoke Mr. Denig, who was still under the influence of liquor, and told him that we must be off—that the Opposition had gone by, and that if they could travel I did not see why we should not. When the chief saw that I was determined to leave, he remarked that it would be well for us to go; that a certain Indian was expected from the fort with a large keg of whiskey, and that it would not be well for us to remain in camp

while they were drunk; for, as he knew, we had to
leave Mr. Denig behind. The mules were soon
harnessed up, and into the hard storm we started,
with but one Indian, who was my guide. It was an
awful day; we could see no distance in any direction,
floundered in deep snowdrifts, and knew not where
to go for timber. But our guide was a good one,
who brought us to a small cluster of scrubby elms.
The snow had drifted so deep that we could find no
dry wood and had to go to bed without a fire. We
made ourselves as comfortable as we could by dig-
ging holes in the snow for shelter. We were then
only a little distance from the meat-pen, where Mr.
Denig was to stop, and reached it early next day.
Mr. Denig wanted me to remain with him over night,
but as he had to make a liquor trade, and I did not
wish to be serenaded, I declined his kind offer. Having packed the contents of my sled on my two mules,
and left the sled, which I found to be a nuisance, I
proceeded on my journey to Woody Mountain.
After this snowstorm the wind changed to a strong,
extremely cold northwester. There were only three
of us—myself; my guide, a young Chippewa; and my
driver, a young Canadian named Piché, which means
pitcher.[8] As my poor Pitcher contained more water

[8] Larpenteur seems to be punning, and perhaps intends
another play on the words " mettle " and " metal." The tru

than whiskey, I was much afraid he would freeze and crack; but he was made of good metal, that could stand heat or cold.   Early this evening we came to a good camping place, with plenty of dry firewood; but it was so intensely cold, and we had to dig so deep in the snow to make a fireplace, that it was with the greatest difficulty we could start a fire.   But we succeeded at last in making a comfortable camp—the best one we had had since we left the fort.   A little while after this we were sitting at a good supper of dried buffalo meat, a few hard-tacks we had saved, and a strong cup of coffee.   After supper arrangements were made for sleeping, as a bedroom had yet to be cleared out, in a deep snowdrift, where my friend Pitcher was to be my bedfellow.   We proceeded to excavate, and soon had ourselves buried alive in the snow.   I believe this was the coldest night I ever felt.   The guide got up first, to make a fire, to the delight of Pitcher and myself.   A breakfast much like our supper was soon ready, the mules were packed, and we were off again.   We had not traveled more than an hour when the wind rose, and the snow began to drift, so blinding us that we could scarcely see.   We had over 10 miles to travel to timber; but, fortunately, we were on the main road, which the In-

name may have been Pichou or Picheau : for this word, see my Henry Journ., 1897, p. 1018.

dians had made so hard, in going from one camp to another, that the drifting snow could not lodge on it; so the tracks remained visible, which enabled us to reach camp in good time. At sunset the wind fell, and we had an easy time in making preparations for our last night out. There being no road between this place and the Indian camp, which was 20 miles off, over level prairie, and wishing to reach the camp in good time, we made an early start next morning.

The day was clear, cold, and calm. In my small outfit I had about five gallons of alcohol, in two kegs of three and two gallons, neatly packed in the bales of goods. I thought this quantity would be too much to bring in camp at once and concluded to cache one of the kegs on the road, for I knew it would be impossible to keep it concealed in the Indian lodge. In order to do this my guide must be dispatched ahead, for I did not think he could be trusted. So, when we got within about five miles of the camp, I remarked to him that I wished him to go on into camp and tell Broken Arm,[9] the chief of the Crees, that I wished him to prepare me a large lodge and make ready for a big spree to-night. To this proposition the guide readily

[9] One of this name appears in Boller, p. 121, but he is given as an Assiniboine, not Cree. "A party of thirty Assinniboines arrived to visit the Gros Ventres. The new-comers have been sent from a camp known as 'the band of Canoes,' by the chief, 'Broken Arm,'" etc.

consented, and, having pointed out the direction of the camp, he left on a dog-trot. As soon as he was out of sight and we had reached a place that my friend Pitcher would be sure to find again, we cached the smaller keg in a snowbank and resumed our journey.

We had made but a few miles when we came in sight of Indians; but, as we could see no lodges, we presumed they were Indians returning from a hunt. We soon discovered men, women, and children; still no camp, and the prairie looking level as far as the eye could reach. We could not imagine what this meant, and were not relieved of our uneasiness till some of the bucks came running up and told us that there was the camp, pointing to a deep valley. Having gone about half a mile we came to a precipice, on the north of which the Indians were camped, near the bottom. It was an awful place; I could not imagine how they could stand such a place without freezing, for the sun did not reach them more than two hours out of the twenty-four. " Now," said I, to my friend Pitcher, " we are north of north here." " Yes, sir," said he, " and we'll freeze. I can't see what made them d——d Indians camp here." For the first time my good Pitcher was overflowing with bad humor, and indeed I did not blame him, for the prospect of staying in such a hole was anything but encouraging.

But there was no alternative; we had to enter the lodge—a large double one—which we found already prepared for our reception. After our mules were unpacked and our baggage was arranged, a kettle of boiled buffalo tongues was brought in; a strong cup of coffee was made from our own stores, and we took supper alongside a good fire, after which symptoms of good humor returned.

Being now ready for operations, I sent for water, telling the Indians it was to make fire-water, and it was not long in forthcoming; the news circulated through the camp, and before I was prepared to trade the lodge was full of Indians, loaded with robes, ready for the spree. The liquor trade commenced with a rush, and it was not long before the whole camp was in a fearful uproar; but they were good Indians, and there was no more trouble than is usual on such occasions. This was the first time that I ever felt snow-blind; during the spree, which lasted the whole night, I complained considerably of sore eyes, attributing it to the smoky lodge. They told me the lodge did not smoke, except at the place where it ought to, and said I must be getting snow-blind. This I found to be the case, and, though I was soon over it, it was bad enough to be extremely painful. By morning I had traded 150 fine robes, about all there were dressed in the camp, and during the day I traded 30

more for goods.   I then feared no opposition, as their
robes were nearly all traded—that is, the dressed ones.
We had plenty of leisure after that, but tremendously
cold weather.   It frequently happens in that part of
the country, that, after a clear, calm morning, a cloud
rises in the northwest about ten o'clock, and in a very
short time a tremendous snowdrift [10] comes on, which
lasts all day; but the weather generally becomes calm
at sunset, turning very clear and cold.   Such weather
we were blessed with most of the time we remained
there, which was about six weeks.   Imagine the
pleasant time we spent in camp under that steep
hill, where I am certain the sun did not shine more
than 24 hours altogether during those six weeks.

[10] It will be observed that Larpenteur does not use the word
" blizzard " for what he describes; but that is what he means.
The word is recent; Dr. Matthews tells me he did not hear it
applied to a storm until after he left Dakota, where he resided in
1865–72; but if I remember rightly, it was in common use when I
was Post Surgeon at Fort Randall, S. Dak., 1872–73. In Boller's
Among the Indians, written of 1858–66, a Dakota blizzard is
called "pouderie "and " poudérie." Either of these forms is pretty
bad French, but the root of the word is *poudre*, powder, and
perhaps it is a corruption of *poudrerie*, powder-mill—the force of
which will be appreciated by anyone who has had a blizzard
burst upon him.   The best explanation of the word " blizzard "
will be found in the Century Dict.   It seems to have first meant
a rattling volley or discharge of fire-arms, then something likened
to such, as a howling spree, and finally fixed itself as the name of a
furious snowstorm.   The word has no etymological history.

The third day after we arrived I sent my Pitcher to see how the mules were getting along; the Indians had them in their charge, but I wanted to know their actual condition from a surer source during such intensely cold weather. The Pitcher was so benumbed that he was unable to tell the news on his return until he had warmed his mouth, which appeared so stiff with cold that he could not move his jaws; but I could see in his countenance that something was wrong. Being anxious to learn what the matter was, and giving him scarcely time to thaw out, I said, " Well, Pitcher, how are the mules?" " Ha! the mules both froze dead—one standing up, the other down. My good fat white mule standing up—thought she alive, but she standing stiff dead." By this time his jaws had got limber, and he made them move at a great rate, with some mighty rude expressions in regard to the place where we were. When well warmed up he began to crack a smile again, and all went well until a couple of days afterward, when I found him so much out of humor one morning that I thought surely my poor Pitcher must be broken, or at least badly cracked. When breakfast was served by the wife of Mr. Broken Arm, the great chief of the Crees, who had been to Washington, Pitcher would not partake. " What is the matter, Pitcher," said I, " are you sick? Why not have some of this good fat buffalo meat?" "Not much the matter," he replied; "I will tell after a while "— fearing perhaps that the story he had to tell would not agree with my digestive organs. Some time after that, when the things were removed, dishes washed up, and the cook had gone out, my Pitcher poured out his story. "Mr. Larpenteur," he said, "if you please, after this I will do our cooking." "Why so," said I. "Why, sir, because that enfant de garce— that old squaw is too dirty. Sacré! She scrape the cloths of that baby of hers with her knife, give it a wipe, cut up the meat with it, and throw into the kettle. This morning I see same old crust on the knife—that what the matter—too much for me." After this explanation I was no longer surprised at poor Pitcher's looking so broken; and if my digestive powers had not been strong, as they have always proven to be, I am afraid my own breakfast would have returned the way it went; but with me, whenever the meat-trap was once shut down it was not easily opened again, and things had to take their natural course.

Shortly after the death of our two mules, I traded a pony of an Indian, and Pitcher would now and then go to see how the animal stood this latitude. Then the time came when I thought the Indians might have robes enough dressed to raise a frolic;

so one morning I sent for the keg of alcohol
I had cached on the road.   Not wishing the Indians
to know what we were about, on their asking where
my man was going, I told them he was going to look
after my pony.   He delayed longer than they thought
necessary, and they remarked it; but finally he appeared in the lodge with the keg on his back—that
being the kind of a pony he had gone to take care of.
I was soon prepared for operations, and another glorious drunk took place; but the robe trade was light,
only 50 in number.   This ended the business, there
being no liquor and hardly any robes left in camp.[11]

[11] No narrative of fur trading *en derouine* needs moralizing,
to adorn the tale of such an atrocious affair.   But it may be
observed that this story shows up the seamy side of the business
to perfection.   That old transaction we read of, in which a birthright was exchanged for a mess of pottage, was not a worse
bargain than these Crees made with their trader.   The weather
was such that a mule froze stiff, standing up; buffalo robes were
the main protection of the Indians from the killing cold.   Out of
210 robes which Larpenteur says he traded, 180 were secured for
5 gallons of alcohol, on which the camp got drunk twice : the
other 30 were obtained for " goods "—some flimsy cloth and such
trinkets as beads, hawk-bells, red paint, and hand looking-glasses.
" This ended the business," as he says, " there being no liquor
and hardly any robes left in camp."   The per cent. of profit to
the trader in this transaction is unsaid—I suppose it to have been
several thousand, as five-sixths or more of the poisonous liquor
the Indians drank was *water*—for which that proportion of robes
was exchanged, under circumstances which would seem to have
made a single robe a more tangible if not a more valuable com-

I then sent the Indian to Fort Union with a letter for Mr. Culbertson, requesting from him the means to bring back the robes I had traded.   Notwithstanding continued severely cold weather, ten days afterward a party of eight men and 20 horses arrived in camp, in charge of the hunter of the fort, Antoine Le Brun.   Those men had suffered so much with the cold that it was almost impossible to recognize them —noses, cheeks, and eyes all scabby from frost-bite, and so dark from exposure that they looked more like Indians than white men.   Mr. Culbertson's letter was anything but satisfactory, its contents being about as follows: " Larpenteur, I send you 20 horses, thinking them sufficient to bring in your trade; if not, try to get some good Indians to help you; tell them I will pay them well.   From what I can learn some Indians, who are moving north on your route, have

modity than any sort of a birthright.   I am here reminded of a striking passage in Bancroft, Works, xxxi, 1890, p. 276: "Whiskey, as applied to the noble savage, is a wonderful civilizer.   A few years of it reduces him to a subjection more complete than arms, and accomplishes in him a humility which religion can never achieve.   Some things some men will do for Christ, for country, for wife and children ; there is nothing an Indian will not do for whiskey."   Turn it as we may, three things, which have done most to make the Indian what he is to-day, are not the state, the church, and the army—they are alcohol, syphilis, and smallpox.   Truly, " God moves in a mysterious way, His wonders to perform."

said they will steal all your horses; therefore I advise you to take a different route."

Now, what to do? The snow was drifted so deep in all the hollows that I could not possibly take any road but the old beaten one. To go any other way would be at the risk of freezing to death—or at least of losing all my animals in the snow; I preferred to take the chances of being robbed and perhaps beaten on the old road.

Next morning by ten o'clock we were under way, with all my trade. I had some few goods remaining, which I carefully concealed between the packs of robes, so that they could not be seen by the Indians whom we expected to meet; and I kept a few trinkets in sight, to make some small presents, should it be necessary. With much difficulty we made out to extricate ourselves from the awful abyss into which we had plunged when we came to this camp. The morning was clear, but extremely cold, and as we reached the level prairie we perceived the usual cloud, indicating a snowdrift. Not long afterward it came on, so bad that we had great trouble to keep our horses in the track. As the old saying is, "There is no bad wind but what will bring some good." This wind was one of them. We should have reached our camping place in good time, had it not been for this heavy snowdrift. A little before dark, when we came to camp, we were surprised by the barking of Indian dogs, which appeared to be not far off. The country was here very broken, and wooded with small oaks. We concluded that this was the camp of the very Indians who intended to rob us. Owing to the heavy snow-drift, which had lasted all day, they had not discovered us, and we arrived unknown to them. Finding ourselves undiscovered, I told the men to make no noise, build no fires, and early in the morning to go for the horses, as I wanted to be off by the peep of day. Some were reluctant to obey orders, but consented to do so on my telling them they did not know what might happen. Sleeping without any fire, in such cold weather, was certainly a hardship, but I thought it necessary for our safety. Supper was made on a little dried buffalo meat—about all we had. After a long, sleepless night, at break of day the horses were all brought up to pack, and at clear day we were under march. On the first hill we ascended we perceived an Indian with his hand on his mouth, which is a sign of surprise. He called out, " Ho! ho! have you traveled all night?" I answered, " No, we camped at the spring." " Why," said he, " did you not come to our camp? You would have been well off with us —we have meat, sugar, and coffee." I told him that if I had known the camp was so near, I certainly would have gone there. All this time my men were filing by, and as each one passed me I told him to hurry up; that I would remain behind with my pack-horse, and get out of the scrape the best I could. The news soon reached the Indian camp, and in a little while I was surrounded. Their main object was to trade horses, and they wanted me to stop my men. I told them the men would not stop; they were cold, and had gone too far off. " Well," said they, " we have got a few robes we would like to trade." I found from their actions, after my poor excuse for declining the horse trade, that they were not so badly disposed as Mr. Culbertson had represented them to be; yet, if they had got the chance at night, I believe they would have relieved me of some of the horses, if not the whole band. They brought a few robes, which I traded; and not wishing my men to get too far off, I made the Indians a present of what little stuff I had left. When they found I was so generous they let me go in peace, with my good Pitcher, whom I had kept by me.

With much relieved hearts we started double-quick, and soon overtook the party. We found them delighted at our good success, and glad they had followed my advice, saying, " If we had been discovered, we should not have one horse left, and God knows what would become of us." One said, " Did you see that big painted rascal, how he look? Bet you he'd

have mounted one of them "; and, after several such
expressions, it was agreed among them that I was a
first-rate leader.

The day became pleasant, we traveled well, and
came to camp at the meat pen, where we fell in with
two Indian lodges. One of these was that of He
Who Fears his War Club, a respectable and brave
man, who I knew could be relied on. After we had
gotten everything righted in camp, the old fellow
told me to come to his lodge, that he had something
to tell me. As we had little to eat in camp I was in
hopes that I would get a supper out of him, and perhaps something for my men to eat; but I was disappointed in that, for he was as bad off as we were. On
entering he bade me sit down; and having smoked a
few whiffs, he asked me if I had heard the latest news
from the fort. I told him I had learned none since
the news brought to me by my men. " Well," said
he, " something very bad has taken place since, and,
if I were in your place, I would not go to Wounded
Leg's camp; for he has had a quarrel with Long
Knife (meaning Mr. Denig) and your chief (meaning
Mr. Culbertson). They took him by the arms and
legs and threw him out of the fort, and he has sworn
vengeance against the whites. It will not be good
for you to go to his camp, or even in sight of it, for I
tell you he is very mad."

This news struck me pretty hard. I had got out of
one scrape, but was already in another; this was
something else for me to cipher on that night, and if
my stomach was empty my head was full. On my return to camp I was asked what the old fellow had
said; the men suspected that all was not quite right,
so I told them the whole story. " Now we are in a
pretty fix again," said one. " Yes," said another,
" they get drunk with the Indians and fight, but don't
think much of us poor fellows on the prairie," and all
such expressions. One said, " Don't go that way ";
and another replied, " You d——d old fool, what
other way can we go in this deep snow? " Finding
them disconcerted, I said, " Don't be uneasy, boys;
I'll figure out a plan to get through."

Meanwhile two strapping big bucks made their appearance in camp, and, of course, they were supposed
to be horse thieves; but their story was that they were
going to the fort, expecting to join a war party.
Notwithstanding this, a guard was placed over them
and I took care that they should have a good bed in
camp, where they could be easily watched. Early in
the morning all hands were roused up; our thieves
were all right, but one of the old chief's little boys.
about fourteen, had got up still earlier and mounted
one of our best horses. He was seen in the act, but
could not be overtaken. His father, a good man.

was very sorry, and said that the horse would not be lost to the Company. The theft, at this time, was of great importance, as all our horses were getting very poor and weak.

From this place to Wounded Leg's camp was a good level road, about 25 miles, which we expected to make early. Now that all was ready for the move, the boys expressed a desire to know what plan I had to get them through safe. I said to them, " This is my plan: I am going on this road right straight to Wounded Leg's lodge. I know him well; he is a good friend of mine, and I am sure I can fetch him all right. When we come in sight of the camp I will go ahead alone. You can come on slowly; if anything happens to me, do the best you can for yourselves; but if things are all right, I will make you signs to come in." They were apparently satisfied, placing confidence in me, and so we started; but, moving at too fast a gait, we were obliged to leave two horses, which had given out. This made three loads which had been divided on the others; it was very hard on them, and we commenced to think we should be forced to leave some of our robes on the way also.

About three in the afternoon the dreaded camp was in sight. I caused all hands to halt, and told them, " Now, boys, I am going to the camp. When you

get within 400 or 500 yards of it, stop. If you see
Indians coming, not out of a walk, remain until they
reach you; but if they come rushing, make up your
minds that Larpenteur is gone up, and defend yourselves the best you can." Off I started. When I
came into camp I inquired for Wounded Leg's lodge,
which was immediately shown to me. On entering
I found his old woman alone. She felt somewhat surprised, but looked cheerful, and we shook hands. She
had always been a good friend of mine, and I thought
myself pretty safe as far as she was concerned. I
asked her where her old man was. She said he had
gone to the lodge of such a one. I then requested
her to send for him, which she did, and a few minutes
afterward he made his appearance. His countenance
was not calculated to inspire confidence. Having
shaken hands, he sat down and prepared to smoke,
as is customary before conversing. I had to hold my
tongue, but my eyes were wide open, watching the
face of my enemy while he was making ready for the
smoke. To my great satisfaction I thought I could
perceive a change in my favor. The pipe being ready
a few whiffs were exchanged, and time to break
silence came. Upon which I commenced, saying,
" Comrade, I have heard some very bad talk about
you. I was told not to come to your lodge, or to
your camp; that you intended to harm me and my

men. Knowing you to be a good friend of mine, I would not mind that talk, and you see I have come straight to your lodge." His first remark was, "Who told you all this?" On my naming the individual, he said, "He told you the truth. I did say all that. I was very angry at the way in which I had been treated at the big house. But I have thought the matter over, and given up the idea of putting my threat into execution; though I am not pleased yet." I soon found that I was in a pretty fair way of success; yet something farther on my part was to be said. So, knowing the Indian character, and, for one thing, that praise of their children goes a long way with them, I commenced thus: "Now, my comrade, you know that the difficulty you had with those men at the big house was when you were all in liquor. You know very well that you are liked by the whites. You are a chief; you have a son—your only child—you love him. He is a fine boy. Although but a boy, you know that the chief of the big house has already armed him like a chief. Would you do anything to deprive your only child, as well as yourself, of chief-hood? No! certainly not. I know you too well for that." At this speech I heard the old woman groan; and, during the pause which ensued, I observed that I had them both about melted down into my affections. The idea of his boy's being so much liked and respected by the whites took the old man's fancy, and a pleasanter or more cheerful chap could scarcely have been raked up.

" Now," said I, " this is not all. I want my men to come in camp and stay with you to-night, and I want you to go to the fort with me. I assure you they will be glad to see you, and I will see that you are well paid for your trouble." Turning to the old lady, I added, " I will send you a nice cotillion." [12] " How!" said she, which meant "Thank you!" Then Wounded Leg said, " That is all right, but you must not come into this camp; it would not be good for you. We are starving, our dogs also; they would eat up your saddles and the cords of your packs. You had better go to camp in the cherry bushes," which he then showed me about a mile off.

Taking his advice, I started back to the boys, and when near them made signs for them to come on. Meeting me and learning the result of my mission, they could not help laughing at the way I had " buttered the old fool," as they said. We steered our course for the cherry bushes, which we reached at sunset. The wind had changed to the north; it became again very cold, and to save our lives we could

---

[12] A piece of dress goods for women's wear, woven in black-and-white.

not get a fire out of those green bushes.   There was not a stick of dry wood to be found, and a tremendous hard night we had.   Sleep was out of the question, and it was too cold to stand a good guard; the result was that the two bucks, who had followed us thus far, disappeared with two of our best horses, one of which we called Father De Smet, because he had been brought from the Flatheads on that missionary's return from the Columbia.   We were then nearly 50 miles from the fort, which distance would have taken us two days; but now, being short of horses, it would take us double that time.   I found an Indian, whom I knew to be a good traveler, and asked him if he could go to the fort by sunset; he said he could, for he had already done it.   I dispatched him with a letter to Mr. Culbertson to send me more horses, and also some dried meat, as we were starving.   Dividing the loads as best we could, we got under way again, making but slow progress, with Wounded Leg, several other men, and some squaws in company.   We again camped, as we all hoped for the last time: but where was supper to come from? We had not a thing to eat and were mighty hungry. I thought of trying rawhide cords, of which we had a few bundles left.   I got a squaw to cut them up fine and boil them; besides which, as a great favor, I got an Indian dog killed and boiled.   That I knew would be good; and as I could not obtain more than one dog, the cords, if the cooking proved successful, would help to fill up. I am sorry to say that I was defeated there, for the longer they boiled the harder they got, and they could not be brought into condition to swallow. So there was only the dog for supper. I had sent it to a squaw to cook for us, and when she gave it to us some of the boys cried, " Mad dog! mad dog!" Sure enough, he did look like a mad dog; for there was his head sticking partly out of the kettle, with a fine set of ivories, growling as it were, and the scum was frothing about his teeth. After the mirth had abated, and no one offered to dish out the " mad dog," I appointed Pitcher master of ceremonies, thinking a pitcher could pour out soup and hold some of it too. He commenced with great dignity, but some of the boys refused to partake, saying they would rather be excused, and could stand it until they got to the fort. This made the portions so much the larger for the balance of us; the biggest part of the thigh fell to my share, which I soon demolished, and I must say it sat very well on my stomach. But some of the boys began to say the " mad dog " was trying to run out the same way he went in; and some noises heard outside might have been taken to signify that the animal was escaping.

It was no trouble to get all hands up next morning,

but some of our worn-out horses had to be whipped up. When once loaded and warmed up by means of the whip, they could only be made to keep on their feet by the same cruel means, which we were obliged to use pretty lively all the morning. Between the hours of eleven and twelve o'clock we perceived the re-enforcement from the fort, at which a great cry of joy was heard throughout the company. The loads were soon rearranged; each man took a piece of dried buffalo meat in his hands to eat on the way; the march was resumed, all eating and whipping, as there was no time to spare to reach the fort that day. Owing to those double exertions, by sunset we were on the ridge, in sight of Union and of its fine large American flag. This had been hoisted on our return from an expedition which had caused much uneasiness, from the many reports which had made it doubtful whether we could ever get back. We were also in sight of the Opposition, and I afterward heard that Mr. Cotton, on seeing us, said, "Well, Larpenteur was not badly robbed—see what a fine lot of robes he has!" In ten minutes after reaching the ridge we were safe in the fort.

Chief Wounded Leg, like the rest of us, met with a cordial welcome; and as a large trading party had just arrived, a keg of liquor was presented him, to drink with his friends. Among them was a certain

Indian named the Hand, the greatest rascal in the tribe, it was believed, who had retaken two horses from some Assiniboines who had stolen them from the fort, and he had come to return them, in company with us. In some drunken spree he had killed an individual whose relations were in the trading party above mentioned. Fearing that he might be killed, I remarked to Mr. Culbertson that it would not be advisable to let him go out and drink with the other Indians—better let him have a little liquor in the fort, and if he got too troublesome we could tie him. This plan was adopted; and as I was much fatigued, I retired, telling Mr. Culbertson to awaken me in case they could not manage him without me. He got so drunk they could do nothing with him, and insisted on leaving; so the door was opened and the gentleman turned out. Early in the morning, I was again on duty. The doors were still shut; but, being tired of hearing a constant knocking, I went to see who was there. By the sound of the voice I knew who he was, and that he was all right; so I opened the small door. "Here," said the Indian, "I killed a dog last night. Take him in and shut the door." This dog was Mr. Hand, whose corpse had been wrapped up in his robe and bundled on a dog-travaille.[18] So much for him, and we were not sorry, as he was a devil.

[19] For the various spellings and etymology of this word, as well as description of the vehicle, see Henry Journ. i, 1897, p. 142.

Shortly afterward we learned that another individual had killed his own father. I shall have occasion to mention him again. Some time before our return I learned that my interpreter had died about eight days after he reached the fort, complaining of headache. The vulgar said he died of the hollow horn; and others, of the hollow head. My good friend Pitcher, I was informed long afterward, struck for Virginia City, where I hope he became a pitcher full of gold."

[14] Larpenteur puns on Piché's name to the end of the chapter, as we see, but it must be noted that in this last instance he is speaking of something that happened about 20 years after the time to which the rest of the chapter refers. Virginia City and Nevada City, a mile apart on Alder Gulch, in present Madison Co., Montana, were two places which sprung up like magic from the rudiments of the first mining camps of June and July, 1863, as if at the touch of King Midas—that great alchemist whose art transmuted all things into gold. The mining district was first called Fairweather, from the name of one of the prospectors, and Virginia City was first named Varina City, in honor of Jeff Davis' wife; but Unionists would not stand this sign of Southern sympathy, and Varina was changed by some caprice to Virginia before its former name had been generally adopted. See, for example, Langford's Vigilante Days and Ways, i, 1893, p. 352, etc., where will be found the best account extant of Virginia City and Alder Gulch—and indeed I think that anyone who reads it will be likely to finish both volumes of this work, which is one of the most entertaining and trustworthy books ever written on the makers and the making of the West. It cost me a sleepless night, which I have never regretted.

CHAPTER XI.

(1844-45.)

CARNIVAL OF CRIME.

JIM BRIDGER, being a great trapper, and having been told that there were many beaver on Milk river, thought of trying his luck in that direction. He left the mountains with a picked party of 30 men, all good trappers and Indian fighters. Nothing unusual transpired at Fort Union until about the month of November [1844] when Bridger and his men made their appearance, having come from Milk river with the intention of passing the winter with us. Mr. Laidlaw, who was in charge at the time, offered him all assistance he could afford, to make his winter quarters pleasant and comfortable, and so Bridger pitched his camp about half a mile from the fort. But he had been deceived by exaggerated reports of the quantity of beaver that could be had on Milk river, and his hunt had been a very poor one. The main substance of Bridger's conversation was his brave men, his fast horses, and his fights with Black-

feet, till we were induced to believe that, with such a
party to defend us, there would be no danger for us
in case of an attack by Sioux.   At that time such
affairs became quite frequent, and the Sioux generally
came in large parties.   Bridger soon had an opportunity to display the bravery of his men, whom he had
cracked up so highly.   A few days before Christmas
[1844] a large war party made a raid on the band
of horses belonging to the fort, running off six of
them, and wounding one of the guard in the leg with
buckshot.   The alarm was immediately given, and
the braves were mounted to pursue the Sioux.
Bridger's clerk, who had been left in camp, came running into the fort out of breath, scared to death.
"Get up all the men you can!   The Sioux are in camp
—they are butchering us!"   Mr. Denig and I, with
a few men, all we could get, took our guns, and ran
with all our might to render what assistance we
could.   Finding that this was a case in which we had
to be cautious, we went along under the steep bank
of the river till we thought ourselves about opposite
the camp, where we stopped to listen for the cries of
the reported butchering.   Hearing nothing, we cau-
tiously raised our heads over the bank, to see some of
the performance.   Neither seeing nor hearing anything, we came to the conclusion the murderous work
had been done, and determined to go to the camp,

expecting to find people cut to pieces and scalped. To our great surprise we saw nothing—not a sign that any Indians had been near the camp. Now assured that Bridger's brave clerk had lied, we returned to the fort laughing at his fright.

During our absence on this dangerous sortie, Mr. Laidlaw was left alone—that is, without a clerk. I had, in my hurry, taken the key of the store with me, and pressing demands were made for ammunition. Mr. Laidlaw, who was a fiery, quick-tempered old Scotchman, smashed in the window of the retail store. Seeing this, on our entrance, we could not imagine what could have been the matter. No word had been received from Bridger's army, but we expected them to return with the recaptured horses and with scalps flying. But soon, to our great disappointment, came the report that a man had been killed; that a mare belonging to Mr. Ellingsworth,[1] the Opposition book-keeper, had been shot through the hip, and that the Indians were daring the whites to fight. The Opposition, who had seen Bridger's men turn out to fight,

[1] Audubon, Journ. i, 1897, p. 520, date of May 28, 1843, has: "Squires and I walked to Fort George, and soon met a young Englishman. . . His name was Illingsworth; he is the present manager of this establishment." Mr. Illingsworth talked buffalo to Audubon, promised to get him a calf, and was better than his word; for he sent one which Audubon skinned to pickle the hide, and the head of another which Isaac Sprague drew.

had concluded to join them. Mr. Ellingsworth had bought this fine American mare of Mr. Laidlaw, who had brought her here in the fall. An old half-breed Creek was also well mounted, and they both very soon came up with Bridger's party, who had halted at the foot of the hills. When Ellingsworth and the old man approached they saw the cause of the halt; the Sioux were on a hill, making signs for them to come on and fight. By this time their party had been re-enforced, and Bridger's men, not accustomed to deal with such a large force, declined the invitation. The old half-breed, who was clear grit, put the whip to his horse, telling the balance to come on; but only Ellingsworth followed. The Sioux, who understood this kind of warfare, and expected the whites to accept the challenge, had left concealed in a ravine a small body of their party, ready to let fly in case the enemy attempted to come on. As the old Indian went by at full speed with Ellingsworth, the Indians fired a volley, which dropped the former dead off his horse, and wounded Ellingsworth's mare in the hip; but did not come so near killing her that Ellingsworth could not make his escape. The Indians, seeing this, commenced to yell, and renewed their defiance. But the brave party concluded to turn back, somewhat ashamed of themselves. Bridger was extremely mortified, and said he could not account for the cowardice of his men on this occasion. At the funeral of Gardepie—that being the name of the old man—these words were pronounced: " This burial is caused by the cowardice of Bridger's party." This expression, it was thought, would result in a fight with the Opposition; but the discontentment disappeared without any disturbance. In the meantime the Sioux went away, having killed one man, wounded another's mare, and taken six head of horses. Bridger became very much dissatisfied with his men, who dispersed in all directions, and he returned to the mountains.

Before I come to the story of the Blackfoot massacre, which is not yet known, I will explain the manner in which trade was carried on this winter [1844-45]. Owing to the local laws which were put in force, we were not allowed to go into Indian camps to trade; the trade had to be done either at the fort, or at an outpost allowed by the agent. So we had to drum up Indians to get them into the fort, and be on the lookout for trading parties coming in. Being well supplied with horses, which we kept constantly in the fort, we had a great advantage over our opponents, who were deficient in that respect. As soon as our pickets, whom we always kept out, in every direction, made the signs agreed upon, we immediately mounted, and, according to signs understood by us, the required number of horses followed. With our pockets full of tobacco and vermilion, we galloped as fast as we could, in order to get ahead of the Opposition, and induce the Indians to consent to come to our fort. But frequently, whether yes or whether no, their robes were put on our horses, and taken to the fort. When the party was large, and some trouble was expected in bringing in the chiefs, a sled was brought out, having a small keg of liquor placed on it, to treat the gentlemen; and a band of music, bearing the flag, was also in attendance. The instruments consisted of a clarionette, a drum, a violin, and a triangle, besides the jingling bells on the sled, and it was almost impossible for Indians to refuse such an invitation. They laughed with delight at the display, and the Opposition could not " come it over them," as the saying is. Mr. Cotton found himself about as badly used up this winter as he had been last; he learned that he stood a poor show in opposing the American Fur Company, and that it would take Mr. Ebbitt, or any other man, a long time to get a footing in the country.

This winter [1844-45 ?] we learned that Mr. F. A. Chardon had had a fight with the Blood Indians, a band of Blackfeet bearing that name; but no particulars were known until the arrival of the returns. which generally came down the latter part of April or

the first part of May.   At that time I was well informed on the subject by Mr. Des Hôtel,[2] one of the
clerks, in whom full confidence could be placed.

Mr. Chardon, who, as has been stated, was the man
who [in 1843] built the Blackfoot post at the mouth
of Judith river, generally called Fort Chardon, happened to have a man killed by that band of Blood
Indians last [?] winter.[3]   This man was a negro by the

[2] Or des Autel, as the name appears in De Smet's earlier book,
1847, p. 338.   This clerk was at Fort Madison in 1846.

[3] "Last winter," by our reckoning, should be 1843-44 ; but it
appears to have been that of 1842-43.   The massacre was certainly known in the spring of 1843 ; for it is mentioned by
Audubon, Journ. i, 1897, p. 501, at date of May 19, 1843, when
he says : "I forgot to say yesterday two things which I should
have related, one of which is of a dismal and very disagreeable
nature, being no less than the account given us of the clerks of
the Company having killed one of the chiefs of the Blackfeet
tribe of Indians, at the upper settlement of the Company, at the
foot of the great falls of the Missouri, and therefore at the base
of the Rocky Mountains, and Mr. Laidlaw assured us that it
would be extremely dangerous for us to go that far towards these
Indians."   The scene of the atrocity was not Fort Chardon, as our
text leaves us to infer, but the post above Maria's river, variously
called Fort Piegan, McKenzie, or Brulé.   It is probable that
Larpenteur's account is the most reliable one we possess, aside
from the discrepancy in date, which may be rather apparent
than real.   The exact date, to the day, must be known ; but
I have not happened upon the record.

This massacre is narrated somewhat differently by James
Stuart, in Cont. Mont. Hist. Soc. i, 1876, pp. 87, 88 : "In 1842,
F. A. Chardon, who was in charge of Ft. Brule [sic—meaning Fort

name of Reese.   Mr. Chardon, it appears, set great
store by that negro and swore vengeance on the band.
He communicated his designs to Alexander Harvey,
who, wishing no better fun, agreed to take an
important part.   They also got old man Berger
to join them.   The plot was, when the band came to
trade, to invite three of the head men into the fort,
where Harvey was to have the cannon in the bastion
which commanded the front door loaded with balls;
when the Indians should be gathered thickly at the
door, waiting for the trade to commence, at a given
signal the three head men were to be massacred in the
fort, and Harvey was to kill as many others as he could
at one discharge; on which they expected the surviv-
ing Indians to run away, abandoning all their robes

McKenzic, above the mouth of Maria's river] massacred about
thirty [!] Blackfeet Indians. The Indians had stolen a few
horses and some little things out of the fort from time to time,
and Chardon concluded to punish them for it. He waited until
a trading party came in, and when they were assembled in front
of the gate, he opened the gate and fired upon them with a small
cannon loaded with trade balls. After firing the cannon, the
men went out and killed all the wounded with knives. The
Blackfeet stopped trading, and moved into the British Possessions, and made war on the post, and were so troublesome that
Chardon abandoned Brule in the spring [1843], went to the
mouth of the Judith, and built Ft. F. A. Chardon on the north
bank of the Missouri river, a short distance above the mouth of
Judith river, which was burnt up when Culbertson built Ft.
Lewis and made peace with the Blackfeet."

and horses, of which the three whites were to become the owners, share and share alike. But it did not happen quite to their satisfaction; for, through some means, the wicked plot was made known in time for the chiefs to run out of the office and escape by jumping over the pickets. Mr. Chardon was quick enough to shoot, and broke the thigh of the principal chief. Harvey touched off the cannon, but, as the Indians had commenced to scatter, he killed but three and wounded two. The rest quickly made their escape, leaving all their plunder; but saved nearly all their horses, most of which were at some distance from the fort. After firing the shot, Harvey came out of the bastion and finished the wounded Indians with his large dagy.[4] I was told he then licked the blood off the dagy and afterward made the squaws of the fort dance the scalp dance around the scalps, which he had raised himself.

I will conclude this chapter with one more of Harvey's awful deeds. It happened that, while he was at old Fort McKenzie, some Indians, who had a spite against the fort, took it into their heads to kill some of the cattle. One day a party of five chased away some of the milch cows, one of which they shot

[4] So copy, for *dague*, French name of a dag or dagger, of the sort we should now call a dirk or bowie-knife. The word runs in many forms through various European languages.

when they had gone a short distance from the fort. On learning this, Harvey and some others got on their horses and went in pursuit. Harvey, who always kept a No. 1 horse, soon overtook the Indian who had shot the cow, and when he got within a few steps fired and broke his thigh; the Indian fell off his horse, and there he lay. Harvey came up to him, got off his horse, and took his seat near the wounded Indian, saying, " Now, comrade, I have got you. You must die. But, before you die, you must smoke a pipe with me." Having lighted his pipe and made the poor Indian smoke, he then said, " I am going to kill you, but I will give you a little time to take a good look at your country." The Indian begged for his life, saying, " Comrade, it is true I was a fool. I killed your cow; but now that you have broken my thigh, this ought to make us even—spare my life! " " No," said Harvey; " look well, for the last time, at all those nice hills—at all those paths which lead to the fort, where you came with your parents to trade, playing with your sweethearts—look at that, will you, for the last time." So saying, with his gun pointed at the head of his victim, he pulled the trigger and the Indian was no more.

CHAPTER XII.

(1845-46.)

POPLAR RIVER CAMP.

THE steamer made her appearance at the usual time, in June [1845], Mr. Honoré Picotte in charge. As it was customary for all the partners to meet in St. Louis in summer, I was left in charge of Fort Union until one of them returned in the fall. I asked Mr. Picotte what kind of men he had brought up; to which he replied, " First-rate men." " Will they not be apt to desert? " " No," said he, " not one." My fear of their desertion was based on their probably being unwilling to go to the Blackfoot post, on account of the massacre of last [?] winter. The steamer left the same day, in the evening. During the night I was made the father of a fine son. In the morning the artillery was playing, and, in consequence of this, something extra must be done. All hands had a holiday, with the promise of a big ball at night. Scrubbing, washing, and cooking went on all day, and at night the ball opened; it went off peaceably, which

was rarely the case in this place. All hands retired in
good time, and had a good night's sleep. Mr.
Auguste Chouteau, who was clerk and had charge of
the men, came to my room early in the morning, saying, "Mr. Larpenteur, twelve men left last night."
Although I expected some desertions, I did not
think any would occur until the men were notified to
go to the Blackfeet; but they had been persuaded by
some of the Opposition who came to the ball, and being afraid they would have to go, they thought best
to disappear while they could get employment elsewhere. I had still many men left, went on preparing
the outfit, and in a few days all was ready for their
departure. James Lee had been sent for by Mr.
Chardon, who had heard he was a bully and a bravo.
Lee was to go up to the Blackfoot post, and it afterward appeared that he intended to chastise Harvey.
During the outfitting we learned enough to induce
us to believe that a plot had been made to pound
Harvey on their arrival, but not to murder him. Mr.
Chardon was then at Fort Clark, his old station. Mr. Culbertson was in charge of the Blackfoot outfit, with the understanding that he was to
burn down Fort Chardon, and build farther up the
Missouri.

I finally succeeded in getting the outfit all right,
but with a frightened set of men. As they pushed

off a large number of the Opposition men were on the shore, crying out to them, " You are going to the butcher-shop—good-by forever!" But the boys, who felt the effects of a good jigger to which they had just been treated, scoffed at this, and went off finely. After this I had the Crow outfit to start off; but there were plenty of men left for this, and for my own use at the fort. Early next morning Mr. Chouteau came to me again, saying, "Seven more men gone last night." This was rather a striker, but on counting the number left, I found that I could send up the Crow outfit, and went to work at the equipment. The following morning, however, three more had deserted, and others kept leaving, one by one, until I had to abandon the Crow outfit. Desertions continued until I was left with but four men all told. This number being too few to keep the fort in safety until the return of the gentlemen in the fall, I immediately dispatched Owen McKenzie,[1] the son of Kenneth McKenzie, with letters to Fort Pierre, to be

[1] "At the White River post, I availed myself of Owen McKenzie's hospitable welcome, and remained in his log-house with another trader of the American Fur Company. Besides these two gentlemen were two other white traders, who had established themselves in a log-house at little more than gunshot distance," Palliser, 1853, p. 165, writing of 1847-48. The opposition traders were Martin and Frederick, the former a Frenchman.

forwarded thence to St. Louis. Much were they astonished when the dispatch arrived. Men were immediately engaged and sent up by Mr. Denig, who had gone on a visit to his friends this summer. Having so few men with me, the Opposition men became very troublesome; so much so that I had to lock the door on them.

Shortly after the return of McKenzie from Fort Pierre, a party of Sioux came to war on the Assiniboines, and had taken all the horses belonging to the Opposition when the alarm was given. We ascended the bastion to see the performance, but it was all over, and the Sioux made bold enough to sit on the hill, quietly smoking their pipes, in full view of both forts. McKenzie, who was very young, active, and brave, said to me, " Mr. Larpenteur, this is too bad; let us go and exchange shots, and see if we cannot get back some of those old plugs." As I agreed to this, we ran down at once, mounted the two swiftest horses in the fort, and off we went. Bullets were soon flying about us, but we succeeded in recapturing four head of horses, which we generously gave back to the Opposition, and our names went high up among the bucks and squaws who were singing and dancing around the fort.

After this times passed off somewhat more smoothly. Mr. Denig, who had been started up with a new supply of men, arrived early in October [1845], and things became quite lively again. Soon after his return, when we were sitting on the porch one evening, we saw Harvey walking up to the house with his rifle across his arm. At a little distance he stopped to ask, " Am I among friends or enemies here? " Being told that we did not think he was in any danger here, he entered and commenced his story with, " Boys, I came very near being killed." Being asked by whom, he replied, " By Malcolm Clark, Jim Lee, and old man Berger; but the d——d cowards could not do it." Then he pulled off his hat, showing the mark of Clark's tomahawk, with which his head had been broken; and his hand was injured where Lee had struck him with a pistol. Being then asked the particulars, he said that, on learning of the arrival of the boat, he got on his horse to meet it and learn the news, as is customary on such occasions. Having gone about 20 miles below the fort, he saw the boat, and beckoned them to land. As he had been left in charge of the fort, they could not well refuse to do so. As the boat landed he gave his horse in care of the man whom he had taken with him, and suspecting nothing, but glad to see the men, he jumped on board and entered the cabin where the three gentlemen were sitting. He offered his hand to Clark, who said, " I don't shake hands with such a

d——d rascal as you," on which a blow of his tomahawk followed, and then a blow with the butt of a
rifle from Berger.　In spite of all this he would have
succeeded in throwing Clark into the river, had it not
been for Lee, who struck him such a severe blow on
the hand with a pistol that he had to let go his hold
and make his escape.　"I then got on my horse,"
he continued, " and when I arrived at the fort I told
the men my story.　They were much displeased, and
as they did not like Clark, and had already learned
Lee's character, they consented to protect me.　I
told them that I intended to hold the fort and not let
a d——d one in."

To this the men agreed, and preparations were
made for defense.　When the boat arrived no one
was allowed to enter, not even Mr. Culbertson.　But
after hard pleadings Mr. Culbertson, who had always
proved a friend to Harvey, made him agree to give
up the fort, on condition that Mr. Culbertson should
give him a draft for all his wages, and a good recommendation.　On receiving those papers, Harvey left
in a small canoe with one man.

He remained but a couple of days at Union, and,
on leaving, said, " Never mind! you will see old Harvey bobbing about here again; they think they have
got me out of the country, but they are damnably
mistaken.　I'll come across Clark again."

Fort Pierre was then the headquarters of the trading posts on the Missouri; all drafts and papers had to be examined and signed there. The company owed Harvey $5000, and he had to get his draft there for the whole amount. Mr. Picotte appeared somewhat slow and did not come to time until Harvey threatened to pound him, when the draft was made out.

It happened that, when Harvey arrived at Fort Pierre, the most important clerks of the post were dissatisfied with their treatment, and had made up a company in opposition to the American Fur Company. The members of this new organization were Harvey himself, Charles Primeau,[2] Joseph Picotte (nephew of Honoré Picotte), and Bonise, the bookkeeper of Fort Pierre, under the firm name of Harvey, Primeau and Co. Under those agreements, which were not known at the time, Harvey immediately left for St. Louis. There he apprised Colonel Robert

[2] A well-known trader for many years among the Sioux and other Indians, and the same for whom was named Fort Primeau, which in the fifties or later stood about 300 yards from Fort Clark, at the Mandans. Mr. Primeau was born in St. Louis, and had been a clerk in the A. F. Co. when he formed the partnership named above. It lasted a few years, and was then absorbed in the A. F. Co. He continued to serve the latter for a time, and afterward held an appointment as government interpreter. He was living at Fort Yates in 1896.

Campbell of the arrangements, and in the spring
[1846] the company started operations, with a large
outfit, sufficient to establish themselves at all the posts
of the American Fur Company.   Harvey came up to
the mouth of the Yellowstone in the steamer, and
went on to Benton in a Mackinaw with his outfit.

A short time after Harvey left us Mr. Kenneth Mc-
Kenzie arrived to take charge of Fort Union.   He
had left the country six or seven years previously, but
had reserved a share in the Company, on condition
that in case of opposition he would return, should it
be deemed necessary by the members of the Company, and on that understanding he now returned.
This was about the commencement of the meat trade
[of 1845]; on his arrival my charge ended, and I was
reinstated in the liquor shop.   Mr. McKenzie was
pleased with my administration; he found everything
to his satisfaction, and said I had done well, though
I ought not to have left the fort, at a time when I
had so few men, to fight Indians.

The American Fur Company, having always had
more influence in this country than the Indian department, thought they would abolish the local law,
and carry on trade on the old principle, which was
camp trading.   So when the robe trade commenced,
traders were dispersed in all directions.   But Mr. Mc-
Kenzie, like Mr. Culbertson, kept me at the fort un-

til the last. Finally my turn came, and I was sent with a good outfit into a large camp on Poplar river,[3] about 60 miles by land above Union. As a matter of course I took plenty of liquor. I had four men and ten horses—more than I wanted—but the intention was for me to send them back loaded with meat for the fort. A certain Indian by the name of Iron-eyed Dog was known as the greatest rascal and ugliest Indian in the camp; his brother had been killed while camped at the fort by a war party of Sioux, who surprised them in the night. This brother was a chief, called the One who Guards the Whites—a very good Indian for us to have. He was shot in the back, the ball passing through his breast. The Indians, knowing that the whites thought much of him, and believing their medicine might cure him, brought him to the fort from camp, which was not more than 300 yards off. That happened about midnight. Shortly after

[3] Present name of the second considerable tributary of the Missouri from the N., above the mouth of the Yellowstone, Big Muddy being the first such tributary. Poplar river is the Porcupine of Lewis and Clark, ed. of 1893, p. 293, whose Martha's river is the present Big Muddy. The Fort Peck Indian Reservation extends along the Missouri on the N. from Big Muddy, past Poplar, to the mouth of Milk river. Camp Poplar River is the military post and agency at the mouth of the stream whence the name was derived, and there is now Poplar station, near where the G. N. Ry. crosses this river. The distance from Union by trail was as said in text ; by the river it is about 95 miles.

he was brought in his brother, the Iron-eyed Dog, came knocking at the door to be let in; but as many others had knocked, we paid no attention to him. This made him extremely angry, and he swore he would kill me on the first opportunity, for he knew I was the doorkeeper. Such was the character with whom I expected to have to deal in this camp, where I arrived on the third day out from Union.

After I had stored everything properly, I was invited into the lodges of the chiefs and leading men, to partake of a dish of pounded buffalo meat and marrow grease, as is their custom. In one of the lodges, where several Indians had assembled, I was informed that Iron-eyed Dog, whom they call in their language Shonkish-ta-man-zah,[4] had gone to the fort, but was expected back that night, and would be apt to make much trouble, and very likely kill me; but they thought I might be able to reconcile him by talking to him and making him a little present, as usual on such occasions. Knowing the Dog of old, I invited the principal chief to my lodge and gave him what he thought was sufficient; he started off, saying that he, with the others, would do their utmost

[4] Shonk-ishta-maza would be a fair spelling of the name, which is compounded of *shonka*, dog; *ishta*, eye; and *maza*, metal. The individual seems to have been a notable character, for I have his name in print, though I do not find the reference among my memoranda.

for me. This was some consolation, but did not go very far toward making me feel safe.

That night, when the liquor trade commenced, the very devil was raised in camp. Iron-eyed Dog, who had arrived, and all the other dogs, including my life preservers, soon got drunk. There was I, with only four other men, among about 300 drunken Indians, with no alternative but to trust to luck. One stout, fine-looking Indian whom I had never seen before, and who suspected something, took his seat by my side, holding a large war-club between his knees, and kept very quiet the whole time. At first I did not know what he was there for, but soon found out; things were as I suspected and feared. Suddenly in came Iron-eyed Dog in great fury, saying, " Here you are! Do you expect to live through this night—you who would not open the door for me when my brother was killed? Did I not say I would kill you?" He went on like this at a tremendous rate, and then rushed out again. But it seemed to me that he did not like the looks of the man with the war-club, who now and then pressed his hand on my knee, as much as to say, " Be not afraid." Then came two more drunken Indians; one of them named Cougher, and the other an individual who had killed his own father; both had plotted with others to murder me in the lodge and plunder my outfit. But it happened that I had a

good old friend in camp, whose name was the Haranguer, and who made such a fine speech that they
abandoned the idea. This is about as near as I can
interpret it: " What is it that I hear? Brothers and
kindred, do you think you will need your trader no
longer, now that spring is come and trade is over?
You have your fill of everything, and now talk of killing your trader. Where will you go? Go north and
starve? Give away your hunts for nothing? Why
kill this poor white man? What has he done to you?
No, brothers! have pity upon him, upon me; spare
his life." On his saying this, which they understood
to be the conclusion of his speech, a young man got
up and handed him his knife, as a sign of approval,
and so the idea was given up. My war-club man all
this time said never a word, but the repeated appli-
cations of his hand inspired a sense of safety in my
badly frightened heart.

After that came the One Who Killed His Father,
and Mr. the Cougher, when all the liquor was gone,
wanting absolutely to get some more, saying, " If you
have none, make some. You whites are strong medicine. You can make fire-water." Seeing, however,
that I was not " medicine," they insisted on my
giving their squaws some trinkets, and off they
went, saying that they would soon be back.
Then in popped the Dog again, and came at me

with his pipe, saying, "Smoke! smoke! Why don't you smoke? I'll make you smoke—you dog, you." This Indian knew I seldom smoked, and only during some of their ceremonies, so he kept running in and out in this manner, and never left the lodge without threatening to kill me.

At last this night, so long to me, wore away; when day came all was quiet in camp, and I felt as though I had been on board a vessel in a gale which had subsided in a perfect calm. After such a storm my appetite was not very sharp, but we had to get breakfast early, before any Indians came loafing in. A strong cup of coffee was soon ready; this revived me, but the dread of seeing the mad dog again was still heavy on my mind. My war-club man was gone, and I saw no one about me that would be likely to take my part. Iron-eyed Dog soon made his appearance with about 20 of his young men, all armed and painted, and I thought then surely I was gone up. The Dog was quite sober, and said to me, " It was a good thing for you that I got too drunk to come to your lodge once more last night, for I did intend to kill you. Now you must give each of my young men some ammunition, tobacco, and vermilion, a knife, and a looking glass; and give those," he continued —pointing to four or five—" a breech-cloth apiece." This being done, he ordered them to go away; "and now," said he, "give me my present." So I gave him 50 rounds of ammunition —the usual allowance for a big man—eight small plugs of tobacco, one knife, one palette of vermilion, and a breech-cloth. To his squaw who was present, I gave a cotillion of cloth, some beads, and other trinkets. He went off without saying another word and I never saw him again; but what became of him will be made known in the sequel.[5]

The trading being nearly over, I sent to the fort for horses to bring in my returns, and five days afterward eight men arrived with 32 head of horses. Mr. McKenzie advised me by letter to be very cautious on my return, as a party of young men had gone up my way with the intention of stealing the horses; to stand strong guard each night, and, if possible, get some good Indians to come with me. I had all my returns ready to be loaded, and next day we got under march

[5] Larpenteur tells a good story, but we cannot help suspecting that the whole affair was a " bluff," to extract presents by working on the trader's fears. It seems to have been a put-up game, in which the war-club man agreed to take a hand, and play the part of a protector for a share of the swag. It will be observed that he does not appear upon the scene, after his disinterested benevolence. The haranguer's eloquence also appears melodramatic. However, there is no saying what a lot of roaring drunk Indians might have done on such an occasion, which was always liable to lead to bloodshed.

with 35 packs of robes, besides some small furs.   The
second night we reached Big Muddy[6] river, about 30
miles from Union.   This being a place which I
thought dangerous, and likely to be my last camp,
I stood the first guard, with one-half of my party.   I
had taken with me one of the first chiefs of the Indian
camp, with three of his most reliable soldiers, which
made our party rather strong.   About eleven o'clock
I discovered the gentlemanly horse thieves coming
straight into camp; they shook hands, seemed glad to
see us, and after smoking a while laid down to sleep.
Seeing us so well on our guard, they gave up the idea
of robbing us; early in the morning they took their
leave, and glad we were to see them off.   The morning was fine and warm, which enabled us to get an
early start.   We expected to encamp at the Little
Muddy, ten miles above Union; but arriving there
about two hours before sunset, and not liking the idea
of another night's guard, we concluded to push on to
the fort.   After smoking a pipe we resumed our
march, and entered the fort a little after dark.   The
fort was full of drunken Indians, as usual.   Mr. Mc-
Kenzie was extremely glad to see me back, and began to tell me how things had gone on during my ab-

[6] The first considerable tributary of the Missouri from the N.
above Fort Union—to be distinguished from another stream of
the same name below the fort.   Distance 42 m. by river.

sence, saying he was at a loss how to get through with all those drunken Indians, with the traders he had in that shop. Finally he said, " Larpenteur, I am forced to ask you to finish this trade, although I know you must be tired. I have been frequently tempted to go and trade myself, but you know that would never do." Finding the old gentleman in such trouble, although much fatigued I went into the shop after a good supper, traded all that night, finished the business, and got the Indians off next day.

This [1845-46] winter's trade convinced the New York firm of Fox, Livingston and Co. that it was a losing game to oppose the American Fur Company; they came to the conclusion to sell out, and we were again left masters of the country.

THE JOURNAL OF JACOB FOWLER

Narrating an Adventure from Arkansas through the Indian Territory, Oklahoma, Kansas, Colorado, and New Mexico to the sources of the Rio Grande Del Norte, 1821-22.

Edited, with Notes, by DR. ELLIOTT COUES

Plate, 8vo cloth, uncut. $3.00 net

Edition limited to 950 numbered copies, and published uniform with "Forty Years a Fur Trader on the Upper Missouri."

Major Jacob Fowler is a hitherto unknown explorer, whose expedition from Fort Smith to the Rocky Mountains and return to St. Louis has never been heard of before. It is printed *verbatim et literatim* from the autograph MS.

The date of Fowler's expedition is a critical one, immediately following Long's, and fills with new data a page hitherto blank in the history of Western Exploration. It contains the first record of ascent of the Arkansaw from Fort Smith to the site of Pueblo, Colorado, first record of building an inhabited house at site of Pueblo, 20 years before Pueblo was founded, first record of making Sangre de Cristo Pass by an American party, first record of ascent of the Rio Grande to its headwaters by an American party, etc., etc.

A FEW REVIEWS ON THE APPEARANCE OF THIS WORK

NEW YORK TIMES:—

The Journal of this expedition now first presented to the public, is a rich addition to the pioneer history of Western America.

THE AMERICAN, PHILADELPHIA:—

What (Dr. Coues) has already done fully entitles him to the unique and enviable position of historian of the early history of Western North America. His volumes attest his indefatigable energy and zeal in the work, and conscientious painstaking research, no less than his knowledge of the subject and his ability to handle it.

THE ROCKY MOUNTAIN NEWS:—

The value of the work (Fowler Journal) is very largely increased by nearly 180 notes by the editor who is peculiarly well fitted for the work by intimate acquaintance with the subject and previous experience in editing similar books.

THE SUN, BALTIMORE:—

It supplements early Western exploration, and the prior accounts of the disposition, manners and customs of the Arapahoes, Osages, Comanches and others, and is a very amusing display of the real, unadulterated human nature of these pioneers. The spelling is a curiosity, and is given as Major Fowler wrote it down.

AMERICAN HISTORICAL REVIEW:—

The memoranda jotted down from day to day by Major Fowler relate to a world in much of which he was the earliest explorer. They ought to have been published long ago. His experience as a land surveyor doubles the value of his observations. Multitudes in Kansas and Colorado will greet his book with a double welcome.

Made in the USA
Monee, IL
09 May 2023

33362267R00155